Book 2

Literature & Comprehension

Writing Skills

Language Arts
Activity Book

Book Staff and Contributors

Beth Zemble   *Director, Alternative Learning Strategies; Director, English Language Arts*
Marianne Murphy   *Senior Content Specialist*
Alane Gernon-Paulsen   *Content Specialist*
Anna Day   *Director, Instructional Design for Language Arts and History/Social Studies*
Frances Suazo   *Senior Instructional Designer*
Cheryl Howard   *Instructional Designer*
Karen Ingebretsen, Anne Vogel   *Text Editors*
Suzanne Montazer   *Creative Director, Print and ePublishing*
Jayoung Cho   *Senior Print Visual Designer*
Stephanie Shaw Williams   *Cover Designer*
Joshua Briggs, Kandee Dyczko   *Writers*
Amy Eward   *Senior Manager, Writers*
Susan Raley   *Senior Manager, Editors*
Deanna Lacek   *Project Manager*
David Johnson   *Director, Program Management Grades K–8*

Maria Szalay   *Executive Vice President, Product Development*
John Holdren   *Senior Vice President, Content and Curriculum*
David Pelizzari   *Vice President, K¹² Content*
Kim Barcas   *Vice President, Creative*
Laura Seuschek   *Vice President, Assessment and Research*
Christopher Frescholtz   *Senior Director, Program Management*

Lisa Dimaio Iekel   *Director, Print Production and Manufacturing*
Ray Traugott   *Production Manager*

Credits

All illustrations © K12 unless otherwise noted
Waterlily, leungchopan/Shutterstock.com; lily leaf © Videowokart/Dreamstime.com; orange koi © Eric IsselTe/Fotolia.com

About K12 Inc.

K12 Inc. (NYSE: LRN) drives innovation and advances the quality of education by delivering state-of-the-art digital learning platforms and technology to students and school districts around the world. K12 is a company of educators offering its online and blended curriculum to charter schools, public school districts, private schools, and directly to families. More information can be found at K12.com.

978-1-60153-209-1
Printed by LSC Communications, Menasha, WI, USA, July 2019.

Contents

Literature & Comprehension

Writing Skills

Literature & Comprehension

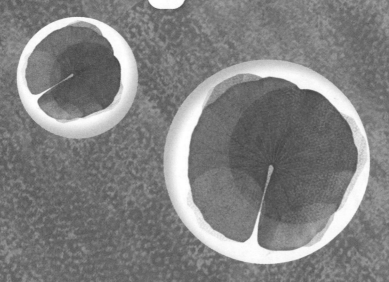

Explore *The First Thanksgiving* (A)
Cause and Effect

Draw a line from the cause to its effect.

Cause	Effect
	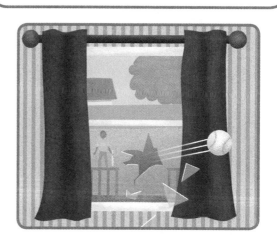

LITERATURE & COMPREHENSION

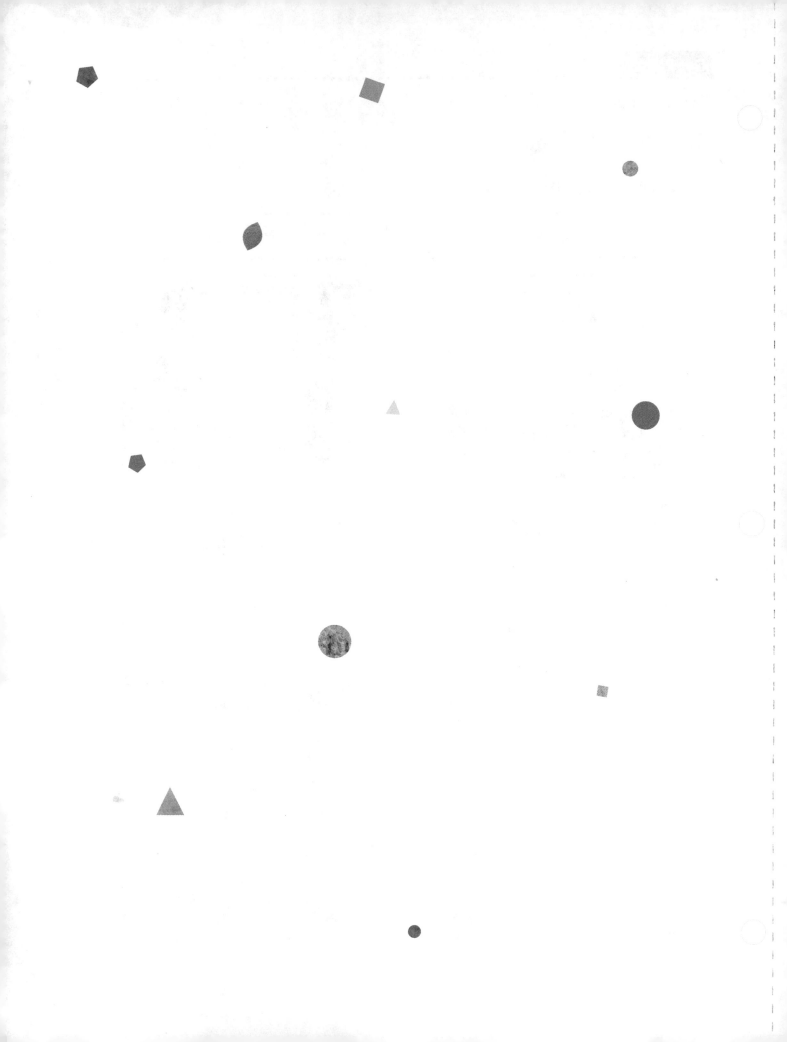

Explore *The First Thanksgiving* (A)
Make Inferences

Fold the page into thirds so that the section labeled ① is showing. Use an accordion, or Z, fold (see the diagram). Use this Reading Aid to read pages 4–25 of *The First Thanksgiving* with students.

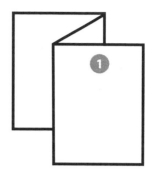

You will read pages 4–25 of *The First Thanksgiving* with students. Stop at the points indicated and follow the instructions.

①

Read aloud page 4.

Ask: Can you tell if the book is about events now or long ago? long ago

Say: I can infer that this book is about events long ago. In the text, I see the year 1620, which is almost 400 years ago. I see more information in the picture—the ships, the horse and buggy, the people's clothes. These things also help me infer that the book is about things that happened a long time ago.

Read aloud pages 6–9.

Say: I wonder how the Pilgrims felt when these things were happening in England. We can't know for sure how the Pilgrims felt, but we can infer it.

STOP **Have students reread** page 9 as they track with their finger.

Ask: How do you think these events made the Pilgrims feel? Possible answers: scared; angry; upset; frustrated; worried   What information led you to infer that? Students will probably refer to the text information about the Pilgrims being spied on and arrested, and having their neighbors turn against them.

Flip over to see ②.

2

Did you use clues in the words of the text or in the pictures to help you make that inference? Answers will vary. Students should indicate that most of the clues came from the text.

Explain that we use both text clues and picture clues to help us make inferences. However, to infer how the Pilgrims felt, students probably relied more on the clues in the text, and then thought about how they would feel in a situation similar to the Pilgrims'.

Read aloud pages 10 and 11.

STOP **Point to** the diagram of the *Mayflower* on pages 10 and 11.

Ask: Where do you think the Pilgrims spent most of their time during the voyage, up on or below the deck? below the deck What clues did you use to make that inference? Students should notice that the picture shows most of the Pilgrims below deck, not on deck.

Why do you think there are so many supplies on the ship? Possible answers: It's a long trip; the Pilgrims had to bring all their food with them. Did you use information from the text or from the picture to make those inferences? from the picture

Open and fold back the page to see ③ .

3

Read aloud pages 12 and 13.

Ask: Why do you think the bread had worms and the water tasted bad? The food and water probably went bad because the trip was long. What do you know from your personal experience that helped you infer this? Students may say that they know food goes bad if it sits around for a long time.

Read aloud page 14.

Ask: How do you think the Pilgrims felt during the voyage? Possible answers: scared; sick Can you "think aloud" and explain why you inferred that? Students might refer to the text information about the terrible storms and the huge waves crashing on the deck. They might say that they would feel scared or sick if they were on a ship during a terrible storm.

Read aloud page 17.

Ask: How do you think the Pilgrims felt when they first saw land? Possible answers: happy; excited; scared Can you "think aloud" and explain why you inferred that? Students might say that after being on the ship for so long, the Pilgrims probably felt happy or excited about land. They may also say that the Pilgrims might have felt scared because the land looked wild and they didn't know if it was safe.

Open and fold back the page to see ④ .

4

Read aloud pages 18–22.

Ask: Do you think the Pilgrims spent most of the first winter in New Plymouth living on the ship or in houses? on the ship How did you infer that? Students might say that the Pilgrims had to build houses before they could leave the ship, but it took a long time to build houses during the winter. Did you use information from the text or the pictures to infer that? the text

Read aloud pages 23 and 24.

Ask: Can you infer how the Pilgrims felt about the Indians? Possible answers: scared; afraid How did you infer that? Students might say that the Pilgrims had cannons and posted guards, so they must have been afraid of the Indians.

Conclude by asking: What kind of information did you use to make inferences as we read this part of the book again? information in the text, in the pictures, and from personal experience

Explore *The First Thanksgiving* (B)
Make Inferences

Fold the page into thirds so that the section labeled ❶ is showing. Use an accordion, or Z, fold (see the diagram). Use this Reading Aid to read pages 26–48 of *The First Thanksgiving* with students.

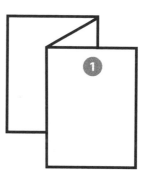

❶

You will read pages 26–48 of *The First Thanksgiving* with students. Stop at the points indicated and follow the instructions.

Read aloud page 26–29.

Say: I want you to think about the Pilgrims' situation at this point in time.

STOP **Have students reread** page 28 as they track with their finger.

Ask: Why do you think so many of the Pilgrims were sick and dying? Possible answers: They didn't have enough food; they didn't have medicine; it was very cold and they didn't have good shelter.

If students have trouble making inferences to answer the previous question, ask the following leading questions.

Ask: At this point, the Pilgrims hadn't started growing food. What do you think they ate during this first winter? Possible answers: food from the ship; birds and animals that they hunted; fish

How much food do you think they could look for, or hunt and fish for, in the hard winter weather? very little   Could this be one reason why so many Pilgrims got sick and died? Yes

The bad weather made it hard for the Pilgrims to build houses. Do you think they had enough shelter to keep them warm and healthy? No

Flip over to see ❷.

2

When you get sick, there is medicine that can help you. Do you think the Pilgrims had medicine to help them when they got sick? No

STOP Have students reread page 29 as they track with their finger.

Ask: Why did the Pilgrims not want the Indians to know how few of them were left? How do you think the Pilgrims felt about the Indians at this point? scared How did you infer that? Students might say that the Pilgrims were afraid that the Indians would attack them if the Indians knew that there were so few Pilgrims left.

Read aloud pages 30 and 31.

Ask: Do you think Samoset was afraid of the Pilgrims? No How did you infer that? Students might say that Samoset walked into the settlement and was friendly, so he must not have been afraid.

Why do you think the Pilgrims wanted to trust Samoset? Students may say that the Pilgrims lost a lot of people during the winter and really needed help. They were probably hoping that Samoset could help them.

If students have trouble making inferences to answer the previous question, ask the following leading questions.

Open and fold back the page to see **3**.

3

Ask: Do you think the Pilgrims felt strong after such a hard winter? Do you think they felt hopeful? No How did you make those inferences? Students may say that a lot of the Pilgrims were weak because they had been sick during the winter. They may say that the Pilgrims didn't feel hopeful or that they felt sad because so many had died.

Do you think the Pilgrims needed help? Yes Is it possible that when the Pilgrims realized Samoset was friendly, they hoped the Indians would help them? Yes

Read aloud pages 32 and 33.

Ask: What did Squanto do to help the Pilgrims? showed them how to survive; taught them how to hunt for deer and where to find berries and herbs; taught them how to plant corn

How would you describe Squanto? Possible answers: kind; friendly; helpful; smart Can you "think aloud" and explain why you inferred that? From their own experiences, students should know that a person who does what Squanto did must be kind, friendly, helpful, and/or smart.

Read aloud page 34.

Ask: Why do you think the Pilgrims wanted to make friends with all their Indian neighbors? because they knew that Indians could be friendly and teach them how to survive

If students have trouble making inferences to answer the previous question, ask the following leading questions.

Open and fold back the page to see **4**.

4

Ask: Did the Pilgrims have a good experience or bad experience with Samoset and Squanto? good

Do you think that the Pilgrims were more likely to trust Indians after their experiences with Samoset and Squanto? Yes

Do you think that the Pilgrims could improve their lives even more if they were friends with their all their Indian neighbors? Yes

STOP Tell students that they will read the rest of the book with you to practice fluent reading. Have students track with their finger and encourage them to chime in and read aloud with you as much as possible.

Read aloud pages 35–48.

Ask: Do you think the Pilgrims would have stayed in America if the Indians hadn't helped them? Why or why not? Answers will vary. Have students give reasons to support their answers.

Conclude by asking: What kind of information do you use to make inferences? information in the text, in the pictures, and from personal experience

Explore *The First Thanksgiving* (B)

Cause and Effect: Pilgrims in America

Complete the chart. Some answers have been given.

	Pilgrims first come to America	Pilgrims after a year in America	What caused the change?
Where they live	on the ship	in houses	
Where they get food	from the ship; what they can find nearby		

LITERATURE & COMPREHENSION

Pilgrims first come to America	Pilgrims after a year in America	What caused the change?
Kinds of food they eat		
How they feel about Indians		

LANGUAGE ARTS GREEN

Explore "Thanksgiving Day"
Sensory Language and Rhythm

Fold the page into thirds so that the section labeled ① is showing. Use an accordion, or Z, fold (see the diagram). Use this Reading Aid to read "Thanksgiving Day" with students.

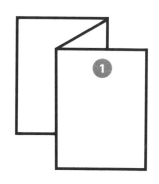

1

You will read "Thanksgiving Day" with students. Stop at the points indicated and follow the instructions.

Read aloud the first stanza.

Have students reread the line "Through the white and drifted snow" as they track with their finger.

Ask: What do you visualize when you hear that line? Answers will vary.

Explain that the poet probably used the words *white* and *drifted snow* to help readers imagine a scene with lots of white snow in the forest.

Read aloud the second stanza.

Ask: Did you hear any words that help you imagine what it would feel like to be riding in the sleigh? Possible answers: *wind: blow; sting; bites*

What do you think the poet wants us to imagine and feel? how cold it feels riding in the sleigh

Flip over to see ②.

3

Conclude by sharing with students your favorite word or phrase from the poem and what it makes you see, hear, or feel. For example, you might like the words *ting-a-ling-ding* because you like the sound of bells and those words help you hear bells.

Ask: Which word or phrase in the poem is your favorite? Answers will vary.   Why is that word or phrase your favorite? Does it help you imagine that you can see, hear, or feel something? Answers will vary.

2

Read aloud the third stanza.

Ask: Were there any words that help you imagine what you would hear while riding in the sleigh? Possible answers: *bells ring; ting-a-ling-ding*

Tell students that the poem has a particular beat that helps us feel the rhythm of the poem. As you read aloud the next stanza, students should listen for the beat and see if the rhythm makes them think of anything.

Read aloud the fourth stanza.

Ask: Does the beat of the poem remind you of anything? Answers will vary. What do you think the poet might want you to imagine when you hear the beat? Answers will vary. Guide students to think about the sound of the horse's hooves as it trots.

Remind students that the poet carefully chose the words of the poem to help readers see, hear, and feel the events of the poem.

Open and fold back the page to see **3** *.*

Explore "Thanksgiving Day"
A Thanksgiving Day Crossword Puzzle

Use the words and picture clues to complete the crossword puzzle.

> snow   wood   bells   sleigh   horse

Clues

1.    2.    3.    4.   5.

```
1.|  |  |2.|  |
  |  |  |  |  |
        |  |
     3.|  |  |  |4.|
        |  |  |  |
        |  |  5.|  |  |  |
        |  |     |  |
```

LITERATURE & COMPREHENSION

Introduce "Digging into Jamestown"
Verbs That Refer to the Past

Cut out the sentence strips and tape them together.

1. The men start

2. building a fort.

LITERATURE & COMPREHENSION

Introduce "Digging into Jamestown"
Verbs That Refer to the Past

Fold the page into thirds so that the section labeled
1 is showing. Use an accordion, or Z, fold (see the
diagram). Use this Reading Aid to read "Digging Into
Jamestown" with students.

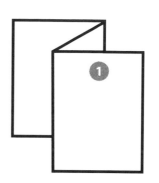

You will read "Digging into Jamestown" with students. Stop at the points indicated and follow the instructions.

·································

Read aloud pages 2 and 3.

Ask: Are the events in the article happening now or in the past? in the past

Explain that we can tell that the events happened in the past because of verbs such as *landed* and *started*. These verbs are written the way we expect for verbs referring to the past, with *–ed* added to the end. But there are some verbs on this page that change how they are spelled instead of adding *–ed* to the end.

STOP **Have students reread** the sentence, "Many people got sick" on page 3.

Ask: What would this sentence say if it was happening now? *Many people get sick.* What does the verb *get* change to if it's referring to the past? *got*

Read aloud pages 4 and 5.

Ask: Which words did you hear that tell us that the events happened in the past? Possible answers: *built; were; came; was; grew; began; moved; stood; became*

Why doesn't the article say, "They builded a church" or "The town growed?" because those verbs change their spelling when they refer to the past

1

2

Read aloud pages 6 and 7.

Ask: Which verbs did you hear that tell us that the events happened in the past? Possible answers: *wanted; was; lived; knew; began; studied; dug; looked; cleaned; found*

Explain that some of the verbs on these pages don't just add –*d* or –*ed* to the end of the verb if the action is in the past. Instead, the verb has different spellings for when it refers to events now and events in the past.

Ask: In the sentence, "So archaeologists began to look for clues," what would the verb *began* change to if the sentence were about something happening now? *begin*

Why doesn't the article say "They digged deep in the ground"? because *dig* changes to *dug* when it refers to the past

Read aloud pages 8 and 9.

Ask: Which verbs did you hear that tell us that the events happened in the past? Possible answers: *found; made; dug; were; brought; needed*

Explain that the verb *brought* in the sentence, "They brought money," tells us about something in the past. But, if the story were happening now, the sentence would say, "They bring money."

Open and fold back the page to see **3**.

3

Read aloud pages 10 and 11.

Ask: Which verbs did you hear that tell us that the events happened in the past? Possible answers: *traded; hoped; was; began; did; found; had; used; wore; made; gave*   Can you use the verb *made* in a sentence? Answers will vary.

Read aloud pages 12 and 13.

Ask: Which verbs did you hear that tell us that the events happened in the past? Possible answers: *came; found; used; hunted; ate; worked; liked; played*

What are some of the verbs on these pages that add –*d* or –*ed* to the end of the verb when they are referring to the past? Possible answers: *used; hunted; worked; liked; played*

The verb *ate* has a different spelling when it refers to something happening now. What would we change *ate* to if the events of the article were happening now? *eat* or *eats*   Can you use the verb *ate* in a sentence? Answers will vary.

Open and fold back the page to see **4**.

4

Read aloud pages 14 and 15.

Ask: Which verbs did you hear that tell us these events happened in the past? Possible answers: *found; put; said; brought; passed; went; took*

What would we change the verb *went* to if the story were happening now? *go* or *goes*

Conclude by asking: Which kind of words in the article tell us when the events are happening? the action words; the verbs   What are some of the verbs in this article that help us determine that the events happened in the past? Answers will vary. Students can refer to any of the verbs in the text.

Can you point to a verb in the article that adds –*d* or –*ed* to the end when it refers to the past? Answers will vary.   Can you point to a verb in the article that doesn't just add –*d* or –*ed*, but instead changes its spelling when it refers to events in the past? Answers will vary. Students should point to a verb with an irregular past tense.   Can you make up a new sentence that uses that verb? Answers will vary.

If time allows, have students demonstrate their understanding of sentence structure. Cut apart the sentence on the sentence strip so that each word is separate. Mix up the words and then have students rebuild the sentence with the words in the correct order.

Explore "Digging into Jamestown"
"Digging into Jamestown": Sequence

Fold the page into thirds so that the section labeled **1** is showing. Use an accordion, or Z, fold (see the diagram). Use this Reading Aid to read "Digging into Jamestown" with students.

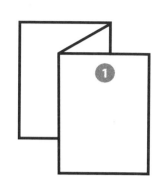

1

You will read "Digging into Jamestown" with students. Stop at the points indicated and follow the instructions.

Read aloud pages 2 and 3

Ask: Did you notice a reference to a date?
Yes   What date does the article mention?
May 1607

Ask: What is the first important event in the article that happened in May 1607? Possible answers: a boat landed in the New World; 104 men and boys from England landed in the New World; some of the first English settlers in American landed in the New World

STOP **Have students reread** the first paragraph on page 3 as they track with their finger.

Ask: What did the settlers do right after they landed in the New World? started building a fort

Read aloud pages 4 and 5.

Ask: What words did you hear that signal the order of events? Possible answers: soon; then; at last

STOP **Have students reread** the second paragraph on page 4 as they track with their finger.

Flip over to see **2**.

②

Say: The first sentence of this paragraph says, "More settlers came from England." The signal word *soon* is right after that sentence. This tells me that Jamestown was full of families after more settlers came from England.

Ask: Which happened first: People began to leave Jamestown, or settlers built towns near Jamestown? Settlers built towns near Jamestown.

Read aloud page 6.

Say: I noticed the signal word *then* after the sentence that says the archaeologists studied old papers to learn where Jamestown was. So I know that the order of events is, first archaeologists studied older papers, and then they started a dig.

Read aloud pages 8 and 9.

Ask: What did the archaeologists find after they started the dig? Possible answers: the walls of the fort; houses; wells; shops

Read aloud pages 10–13.

Explain that these pages give descriptions of what archaeologists have found buried in Jamestown and what those artifacts tell us about the Jamestown settlers. These pages don't tell us a sequence of events. However, we should pay attention to the next pages because they describe a sequence of events related to a specific artifact.

Open and fold back the page to see **③**.

③

Read aloud pages 14 and 15.

Explain that when the article says "in the 1600s," that means the years from 1600 to 1699. We don't know exactly when the tag was put on a box and sent to Jamestown, but we know it happened at some point in that time period. But even if we can't tell exact years of events, page 14 does have clues about the order in which things happened.

STOP **Have students reread** page 14 as they track with their finger.

Ask: Besides the phrase "in the 1600s," what words or phrases did you hear that can help us figure out the sequence of events? Possible answers: *hundreds of years; then; soon*

Which happened first: Archaeologists started their dig, or archaeologists found the tag? Archaeologists started their dig.

Conclude by asking: When an article has the important events described in the order in which they happened, how do we say the article is organized?: in sequence

What are some of the clues in this article that helped us figure out that most of the article is written in sequence? Possible answers: It has years in it; it has signal words such as *soon, then,* and *at last*; it talks about important events in the order that they happened.

Explore "Digging into Jamestown"
What Would Archaeologists Find?

Fill in the chart. Compare artifacts from Jamestown to artifacts that might be found in your neighborhood.

Place	Jamestown	My neighborhood
Kinds of buildings		
Kinds of tools		
Kinds of food		
Other artifacts		

LITERATURE & COMPREHENSION

Introduce "Colonial Kids"
"Read" Visual Information

Fold the page into thirds so that the section labeled **1** is showing. Use an accordion, or Z, fold (see the diagram). Use this Reading Aid to read "Colonial Kids" with students.

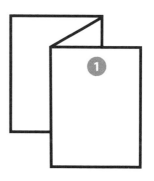

You will read "Colonial Kids" with students. Stop at the points indicated and follow the instructions.

Have students look at the photos on pages 16 and 17.

Ask: Before we even read, can you tell if the article is about events now or long ago? long ago   How can you tell? Students may say that the children's clothes and the ship are from long ago.

Read aloud page 17.

Ask: According to this page, in what two places did children live in the New World? Plymouth, Massachusetts; the Virginia colony

STOP **Point to** the map on page 17. Explain that the map can give us more information about where colonial children lived.

Ask: Was the Plymouth colony by the ocean or in the mountains? by the ocean   Did the words of the article tell us that? No   How can you tell Plymouth was by the ocean? The map shows *Plymouth* written in the water, and there's a dot right by the water that stands for Plymouth.

Flip over to see **2**.

1

2

Read aloud the text on pages 18 and 19 but not the labels in the illustrations.

Ask: Did the text we just read tell us the names of all the different clothing items that colonial children wore? No   What should we look at to learn more about colonial children's clothes? the illustrations with labels

What did colonial children wear that's the same as what you wear today? What did they wear that's different from what you wear today? Answers will vary.

Read aloud pages 20 and 21.

Ask: What are some of the foods the Pilgrims ate? Possible answers: meat; fish; porridge; bread; vegetables; fruit

From the photos, can you tell if there's something else the Pilgrims ate that wasn't mentioned in the text? lobster

Read aloud pages 22 and 23.

What did colonial children learn to read from? the Bible; a hornbook

Open and fold back the page to see **3**.

3

STOP Point to the hornbook on page 22.

Ask: What is this? a hornbook   Colonial children used hornbooks to learn how to read. Why do you think there's a picture of a hornbook here? to help us understand what it looks like

STOP Have students look at the photos on pages 24 and 25.

Ask: Before we even read, can you tell me the kinds of chores young colonial children did? gathered wood; fed animals; got water

Read aloud pages 24 and 25.

Ask: Do you think it was easy or hard to carry water and wood? Did you decide on your answer because of what we read or what you see in the pictures? Answers will vary.

Read aloud page 27.

Ask: What were some of the games that colonial children played? Possible answers: tic-tac-toe; checkers; hide-and-seek; leapfrog

Were colonial girls' dolls the same as or different from most dolls today? different   Did you figure that out from the text or the pictures? pictures

Open and fold back the page to see **4**.

4

STOP Have students look at the illustration of colonial children playing games on page 26.

Ask: Do you think colonial children did other fun activities and played other kinds of games in addition to what the text says? Yes   What are some of the children in the illustration doing? Possible answers: walking on stilts; swinging; bowling

Conclude by asking: What are some of the visual features we find in informational text? Possible answers: photos; illustrations; maps

Why is it helpful to see photos and illustrations along with the words we read on the page? It makes it easier to remember information; it can give us a better understanding of what we read.

Explore "Colonial Kids"

"Colonial Kids": Compare and Contrast

Fold the page into thirds so that the section labeled ① is showing. Use an accordion, or Z, fold (see the diagram). Use this Reading Aid to read "Colonial Kids" with students.

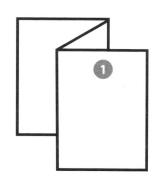

①

You will read "Colonial Kids" with students. Stop at the points indicated and follow the instructions.

Read aloud page 17.

Explain that this page is the introduction to the article. The introduction tells us that this article is going to talk about what life was like for colonial children.

Say: I heard some words on these pages that tell me that the article is written to compare and contrast. That means that there will be information about how things are alike and different.

Read aloud pages 18 and 19.

STOP **Have students reread** page 18 aloud as they track with their finger.

Ask: Which words did the author use that let us know the article compares and contrasts things? Possible answers: *same; different; differently*

Say: I can see that the author is comparing and contrasting what colonial boys and girls wore. But I notice that the author also tells us that colonial children's clothing was different from what we wear today.

Ask: What are some things that you wear that are different from what colonial children wore? Answers will vary.

2

Read aloud pages 20 and 21.

Say: I didn't hear anything on these pages that says exactly how colonial boys and girls were alike or different. But I did notice something that is different about the names of colonial children's meals and our meals.

STOP **Have students reread** the first paragraph on page 20 aloud as they track with their finger.

Ask: When did colonial children eat their main meal of the day? *in the middle of the day* What did they call that meal? *dinner* What do we call our meal in the middle of the day? *lunch*

Read aloud pages 22 and 23.

Say: These pages describe how colonial children learned.

Ask: Did the author say that there was anything different about how colonial boys and girls learned? *No*

Say: So these pages describe something that is the same about colonial boys and girls.

3

Ask: What did a colonial child learn to read from? *the Bible; a hornbook* How is that different from the materials you learn to read from? Students may say that they use books, computers, or other reading materials that are typically used today.

Who taught colonial children? *their parents* Is that the same as or different from who teaches you? Answers will vary.

Read aloud pages 24 and 25.

Ask: Do these pages compare and contrast colonial boys and girls? *Yes*

Can you name one chore that was the same for young boys and girls? Possible answers: carrying wood; carrying water; taking care of chickens

Can you name one chore that older girls did that older boys did not do? Answers will vary. Accept any chore named on pages 24 and 25 that was different for girls and boys.

Read aloud page 27.

Ask: Did colonial children play some of the same games that you play today? *Yes* What are some of the games they played that are the same as today? Possible answers: tic-tac-toe; checkers; hide-and-seek; leapfrog

Open and fold back the page to see **3** *.*

4

STOP **Have students reread** the third paragraph on page 27 aloud as they track with their finger.

Ask: Colonial children did play some of the same games as today, but there was something different about them. What was different? *the names*

What did colonial children call the games they played? Possible answers: Tic-tac-toe was called *naughts and crosses*; checkers was called *draughts*; hide-and-seek was called *all hid*; leapfrog was called *hop frog.*

Conclude by asking: How did the author organize the information in the article "Colonial Kids?" *to compare and contrast*

If you compare and contrast things, what are you describing? *how they are the alike and different*

What are some of the words we might find in an article that is written to compare and contrast? Possible answers: *same; different; alike*

Open and fold back the page to see **4** *.*

Explore "Colonial Kids"

Ask and Answer Questions About Colonial Life

Complete the chart. Some answers have been given.

Question	Where to find answer	Answer
Name of settlement Where did colonists live in the New World?	*The First Thanksgiving*; "Digging into Jamestown"; "Colonial Kids"	
Food What did colonists eat?		

LITERATURE & COMPREHENSION

	Question	Where to find answer	Answer
Clothes			
Chores			
Tools			

LANGUAGE ARTS GREEN

Explore *Here Comes the Parade!* (A)

"What a Parade!" and "Look What I Found!": Repair Comprehension

Fold the page into thirds so that the section labeled ❶ is showing. Use an accordion, or Z, fold (see the diagram). Use this Reading Aid to read "What a Parade!" and "Look What I Found!" in *Here Comes the Parade!* with students.

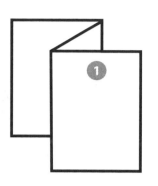

❶

You will read "What a Parade!" and "Look What I Found!" in *Here Comes the Parade!* with students. Stop at the points indicated and follow the instructions.

Read aloud the story until the page that begins "I can't wait to see the clowns, Jade!"

Say: Two characters are speaking out loud on this page.

Ask: Do you remember some of the clues that tell us a character is speaking out loud?

Possible answers: quotation marks; certain words, like *said, yelled, answered, asked*

Can you show me where Jordan is speaking?
Can you show me where Justin is speaking?
Answers will vary.

Read aloud the next page.

Say: I'm a little confused about who is saying what on this page, especially this line here that says, "Sure you do!" Right before that line, I see *Justin said.* But right after, I see *said Jordan.* Let's use our prior knowledge to help us figure it out.

Ask: Based on what we've learned about the characters on the previous page, who is more excited to see the clowns, Justin or Jordan? Jordan

Flip over to see ❷.

2

STOP **Have students reread** from the beginning through the sentence, "Justin still looked worried."

Say: I'm a little confused about who said, "They're funny!" I'm wondering if it was Justin, because his name is right here after the exclamation. Let's try rereading this page more slowly and carefully to figure it out.

STOP **Have students reread** the page as they track with their finger.

Say: Now I see that Justin said, "I don't like clowns," and right after that, Jordan said, "Sure you do! They're funny!"

Read aloud the page that begins "Look What I Found!" through the page that ends, "'There's a ton of money in it,' he said."

Say: Look at this: "Jordan, Jade, look!" Justin held up a wallet. I'm a little confused because I see quotation marks, so I know someone is talking, but I don't see anything that tells me who is talking. I don't see "said Jordan" or "said Justin" or "said Jade." How do we know who is talking? Can you reread the page so we figure out who is speaking?

Open and fold back the page to see **3** .

3

STOP **Have students reread** the page as they track with their finger.

Ask: Do we know who was speaking? Yes Who was speaking? Justin How do we know? The speaker called out to Jordan and Jade; the only other person there is Justin, so it's Justin who is speaking.

Read aloud the next page.

Say: I'm confused about who says "There's a ton of money in it." Can you reread the page and then "think aloud" to help me figure out who is speaking at the end of the page?

STOP **Have students reread** the text as they track with their finger.

Ask: Do we know who was speaking? Yes Who was speaking? Jordan How do we know? The text says "he said." Jade is a girl and Jordan is a boy, so it's Jordan who was speaking.

Open and fold back the page to see **4** .

4

Conclude by asking: How can we tell that somebody is speaking out loud in a story? Possible answers: quotation marks; words like *said, asked, shouted, yelled, answered*

Can you show me quotation marks somewhere in the story? Students should point to quotation marks anywhere in the text.

What can you do if you realize that you're confused about something you just read? Possible answers: You can reread; you can ask yourself a question and then reread; you can think about your prior knowledge and then reread.

Explore *Here Comes the Parade!* (B)

"Big Dreams": Read with Expression

Fold the page into thirds so that the section labeled **1** is showing. Use an accordion, or Z, fold (see the diagram). Use this Reading Aid to read "Big Dreams" in *Here Comes the Parade!* with students.

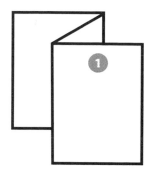

1

You will read "Big Dreams" in *Here Comes the Parade!* with students. Stop at the points indicated and follow the instructions.

Read aloud from the page that begins with "Big Dreams" through "…Ducks shirt, too."

Tell students that as they read the rest of the story, they should look for punctuation marks and other hints about how to read with expression.

STOP Point to the first line, "Can we keep it?" asked Justin.

Ask: What punctuation mark do you see at the end of this sentence? a question mark

Ask: How do you think Justin felt? Possible answers: excited, happy Because of how Justin felt, and because there's a question mark at the end of the sentence, how do you think Justin said "Can we keep it?" Answers will vary.

Have students read aloud both pages as they track with their finger. Make sure they read with the expression that the question mark calls for.

Flip over to see **2**.

4

3

Conclude by asking: Can you show me a question somewhere in this chapter? Students should indicate any question in the chapter. How should our voices sound when we read a question out loud? Our voices should rise at the end.

2

Read aloud the next two pages, beginning with "And I would like a new bracelet...."

Tell students that on this page Jade is dreaming about what she'd buy with the money, so as students read aloud, they should think about how Jade would speak.

Read aloud the next two pages, beginning with "Jordan looked at Jade...."

STOP **Point to the second line, "What should we do?" and ask:** Can you read this line the way you think Jordan said it? Answers will vary. Be sure students use appropriate expression.

Point to the two lines at the top of the next page and ask: How do you think Justin said these words? Guide students to recognize that Justin was excited to keep the wallet and didn't want to return it, so he was probably upset when he said it.

Read aloud the next two pages, ending with "sang along."

Have students read aloud: the two pages, ending with "sang along."

Tell: students that when they read aloud, you want them to practice reading fluently and with appropriate expression.

Open and fold back the page to see **3**.

Explore *Here Comes the Parade!* (C)
Compare and Contrast Characters

Describe Justin and Jordan to complete the Venn diagram.

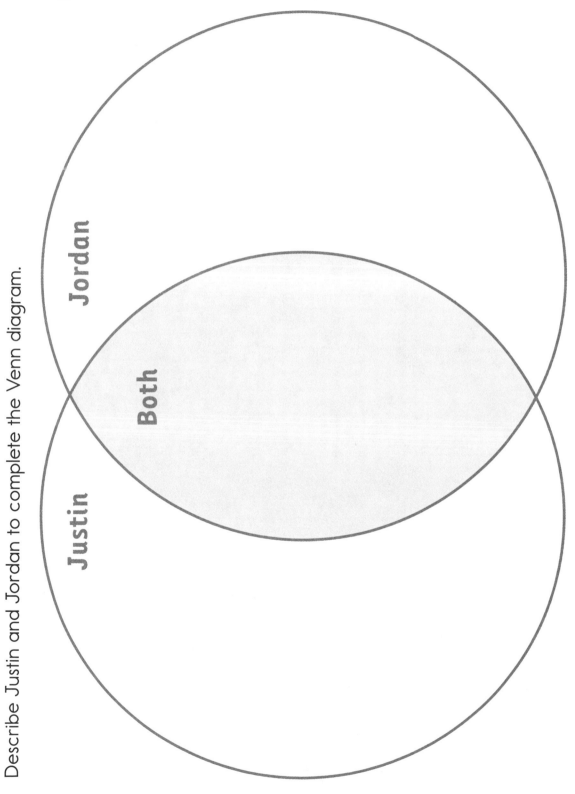

Jordan

Both

Justin

LITERATURE & COMPREHENSION

Explore *Tales of Amanda Pig* (A)
"Amanda's Egg": Questions

Cut out the sentence strips and tape them together.

1. Did you throw it

2. on the floor?

LITERATURE & COMPREHENSION

Explore *Tales of Amanda Pig* (A)
"Amanda's Egg": Questions

Fold the page into thirds so that the section labeled ❶ is showing. Use an accordion, or Z, fold (see the diagram). Use this Reading Aid to read "Amanda's Egg" in *Tales of Amanda Pig* with students.

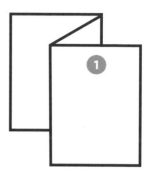

LITERATURE & COMPREHENSION

You will read "Amanda's Egg" with students. Stop at the points indicated and follow the instructions.

Read aloud pages 7–9.

Ask: Did you see any questions on these pages? Yes

What question does Father ask on page 8? "Will you excuse me?"

What question does Oliver ask on page 9? "May I go outside too?"

What should your voice sound like when you read aloud a question? Your voice should rise at the end.

STOP **Have students reread** the questions on pages 8 and 9 as they track with their finger. Make sure that they read with appropriate expression at the end of each question.

Tell students that there are no questions on pages 10–14. When they read those pages together with you, they should focus on reading fluently.

Flip over to see ❷.

❶

3

Read aloud page 16.

Ask: What does Mother ask at the top of page 16? "Did you put it in your pocket?"

Can you read that question aloud the way that you think Mother asked it? Students' voices should rise when they say the word *pocket*.

What question does Amanda ask on page 16? "May I go outside now?"

Can you read that question aloud the way that you think Amanda asked it? Students' voices should rise when they say the word *now*.

Conclude by asking: Can you show me a question mark somewhere on the last page of the story? Students should indicate any question mark on the last page.

What kind of sentence ends with a question mark, a telling sentence or an asking sentence? an asking sentence

If time allows, have students demonstrate their understanding of sentence structure. Cut apart the question on the sentence strip so each word is separate. Mix up the words and then have students rebuild the question with the words in the correct order.

2

Read aloud pages 10–14.

Tell students to look and listen for questions as they read the last two pages of the story.

Read aloud page 15.

Ask: Who asks questions on this page? Mother

What does Mother say after Amanda says that she's all done? "What?"

Do you think that Mother is surprised that Amanda is done? Yes

How do you think Mother's voice sounds when she says "What?" Students should say, "What?" so that they sound surprised.

What else does Mother ask on page 15? "Did you throw it on the floor?"

Can you read that question aloud the way that you think Mother asked it? Students' voices should rise when they say the word *floor*.

Open and fold back the page to see **3** .

Explore *Tales of Amanda Pig* (B)
"The Monster": Make Inferences

Fold the page into thirds so that the section labeled ① is showing. Use an accordion, or Z, fold (see the diagram). Use this Reading Aid to read "The Monster" in *Tales of Amanda Pig* with students.

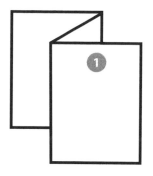

①

You will read "The Monster" in *Tales of Amanda Pig* with students. Stop at the points indicated and follow the instructions.

Read aloud page 28.

Say: Let's try to infer how Amanda is feeling right now. The clues from the story are that Amanda doesn't want to go upstairs, because she thinks there's a monster in the hall.

Ask: How do you think you would feel if you thought there was a monster in your hall?
scared

What inference can you make about how Amanda feels? She's probably scared.

Read aloud page 29.

Say: Sometimes we can use information from the pictures in a story to help us make an inference. Let's look at the picture on page 29.

Ask: Why do you think Amanda says the clock is a monster at night? Students may say that parts of the clock look like parts of a body, such as eyes, feet, or arms. Did you use information from the story or from a picture to help you make that inference? from a picture

Do you think the clock would look scary during the day? Answers will vary.

Flip over to see ②.

2

Why do you think the clock looks scary at night to Amanda but not during the day? Possible answers: because it's dark at night; because Amanda is afraid of the dark   What do you know from your experiences that helped you make that inference? Students may say that things can look scary in the dark, or that they are afraid of the dark.

Read aloud pages 30 and 31.

Ask: Do you think that Father is really too scared to go upstairs? No   Why do you think he pretends that he's scared? Possible answers: He wants Amanda to know that it's okay to be scared; he thinks that Amanda will feel better if a grown-up is scared, too.

Read aloud pages 32 and 33.

Ask: Do you think that Father really wants to scare a monster, or do you think that he wants to help Amanda feel brave? He wants to help Amanda feel brave.   Why do you think that Father wants to help Amanda feel brave? Students may say that fathers like to help their children.

Open and fold back the page to see **3** *.*

3

Read aloud pages 34 and 35.

Ask: Do you think the clock still looks like a monster when Father shines his flashlight on it? Why or why not? Answers will vary. Be sure students justify their answer.

Read aloud pages 36 and 37.

Ask: Do you think that Amanda is sure that the clock is not a monster? No   What information in the story did you use to make that inference? Amanda asks her father, "What if I have to get up . . . and it is very dark and the clock looks like a monster again?"

How you think Amanda is feeling when she asks her father about the clock looking like a monster again? Possible answers: worried; nervous

Read aloud page 38.

Ask: How do you think Amanda feels at the end of the story? Possible answers: safe; happy   How did you make that inference? Students may say that the things Father left will make Amanda feel safe, or that the picture shows Amanda smiling, so she must feel happy.

Open and fold back the page to see **4** *.*

4

What do you think Father means when he says "Just in case" at the end of the story—*just in case what?* Answers will vary. Students may say that Father means just in case the clock looks like a monster again, or just in case Amanda thinks she sees a monster again.

Conclude by asking: What kind of information did you use to make inferences as we read this story again? information in the story, in the pictures, and from personal experience

LANGUAGE ARTS GREEN

Explore *Tales of Amanda Pig* (C)
Who, Where, What

Cut out the pictures, and then glue them onto the story map on page LC 177.

Glue the pictures on the story map. Complete the sentences on page LC 178. Then, retell the story.

Characters	Setting

Title
"Sleeping Time"

Plot

Beginning of story	Middle of story	End of story

Problem and solution in "Sleeping Time": _____

_____

_____

This story reminds me of _____

_____ .

Introduce "Marvelous Mount Rushmore"
Pronouns

Fold the page into thirds so that the section labeled ① is showing. Use an accordion, or Z, fold (see the diagram). Use this Reading Aid to read pages 28–35 of "Marvelous Mount Rushmore" with students.

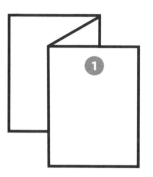

LITERATURE & COMPREHENSION

---

①

You will read pages 28–35 of "Marvelous Mount Rushmore" with students. Stop at the points indicated and follow the instructions.

Read aloud pages 28 and 29.

Explain that the last paragraph on page 29 talks about both Doane Robinson and Gutzon Borglum. Tell students that you are going to reread that paragraph. Say that as you read, you want them to listen for the pronoun *he* and think about which man *he* refers to.

Ask: Which man does the word *he* refer to? Gutzon Borglum

Read aloud the last paragraph on page 29.

Ask: Which man does the word *he* refer to? Gutzon Borglum

Explain that we can figure out that *he* refers to Gutzon Borglum because the sentence that says "Gutzon was excited about the project" comes right before the sentence that says "He had a perfect place to work."

Read aloud page 30.

Ask: Which pronoun did you hear that was used instead of repeating the presidents' names over and over? *he*

Whom does the pronoun *he* refer to in the last paragraph on page 30? Theodore Roosevelt

Flip over to see **②**.

2

Why isn't the pronoun *she* used to refer to Theodore Roosevelt? because *she* refers to a woman and Theodore Roosevelt was a man

How do you know that the word *he* in the last paragraph isn't referring to one of the other men that are discussed on that page? because that paragraph is all about Theodore Roosevelt

Read aloud pages 32 and 33.

Tell students that they are going to reread the paragraph on page 33. As they read, you want them to listen for the pronoun *they* and think about whom *they* refers to.

STOP **Have students read aloud** the paragraph on page 33 as they track with their finger.

Ask: Whom does the word *they* refer to? the four presidents

Explain that we can check whether *they* refers to the four presidents. We can read the sentence substituting *the four presidents* for the pronoun *they* and see if the sentence makes sense.

Open and fold back the page to see **3**.

3

Read the following sentences: "These four presidents played an important part in American history. Soon, the four presidents would also be part of a giant sculpture."

Ask: Do the sentences make sense when we substitute *the four presidents* for *they*? Yes

Say: So we are able to confirm that the pronoun *they* stands for *the four presidents* in the paragraph.

Read aloud page 34.

Tell students that the second paragraph on page 34 has two pronouns. Tell them that they are going to reread the paragraph. As they read, you want them to listen for pronouns.

STOP **Have students read aloud** the second paragraph on page 34 as they track with their finger.

Ask: Which pronouns did you hear? *they, it*

Say: Listen to the following sentences from that paragraph and think about whom the pronoun *they* refers to: "The blasters' job came first. They set up dynamite."

Ask: Whom does the pronoun *they* refer to? the blasters

Open and fold back the page to see **4**.

4

Explain that sometimes a pronoun refers to a thing instead of a person.

Say: Listen to the following sentences from that paragraph and think about what the pronoun *it* refers to: "They set up dynamite. Boom! It blasted away big pieces of rock."

Ask: What thing does *it* refer to? dynamite

Read aloud page 35.

Ask: What pronoun did you hear on this page? *they*

Tell students that they are going to reread the first paragraph on page 35. As they read, you want them to listen for the pronoun *they* and think about whom *they* refers to.

STOP **Have students read aloud** the first paragraph on page 35 as they track with their finger.

Ask: Whom does the pronoun *they* refer to? the sculptors

Conclude by asking: What kind of words does an author use so that the names of people and things aren't repeated over and over in a text? pronouns   Can you point to a pronoun somewhere in the article? Students should point to any pronoun in the article.

LANGUAGE ARTS GREEN

Explore "Marvelous Mount Rushmore"

"Marvelous Mount Rushmore": Time Line

Fold the page into thirds so that the section labeled **1** is showing. Use an accordion, or Z, fold (see the diagram). Use this Reading Aid to read "Marvelous Mount Rushmore" with students.

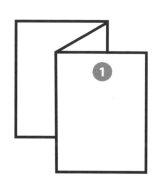

1

You will read "Marvelous Mount Rushmore" with students. Stop at the points indicated and follow the instructions.

Read aloud pages 28 and 29.

Ask: What happened in the 1920s, according to the article? Doane Robinson came up with the idea to carve a sculpture into a mountain.

Explain that when the text says "the 1920s," that means the years between 1920 and 1929.

Write *the 1920s* and what happened on an index card. Set the card aside for later use.

Tell students that pages 30–37 do not have any years in the text. Explain that you want them to focus on reading the pages fluently as they read aloud with you and track with their finger.

Read aloud pages 30–37.

Tell students to listen for years and other clues to when important events happened as they read aloud to the end of the article with you.

Read aloud pages 38 and 39.

Ask: What years did you hear mentioned? 1927, 1941

Flip over to see **2**.

3

Tell students that they will now make a time line by arranging the index cards in order and laying them on a flat surface. Have students read the year(s) on each card and place the cards in chronological order.

Have students read aloud the year(s) and events described on each index card in the order in which they happened.

Ask: What is the first event on our time line? the 1920s—Doane Robinson came up with the idea to carve a sculpture into a mountain.

What is the last event on our time line? 1941—Abraham Lincoln's face was finished.

Conclude by asking: What kind of information did we find in the article that helped us put the events in order? years

What do we call the line that we made out of the index cards? a time line   Why is it called a time line? because it shows when important things happened in time and the order in which they happened

2

What happened in 1927? Workers began carving George Washington's face.

What happened in 1941? Abraham Lincoln's face was finished.

Write *1927* and *1941* and what happened in each of those years on separate index cards. Set the cards aside.

Explain to students that there is a clue to the year of another important event in the text.

Have students read aloud the first three sentences on page 39 as they track with their finger.

Ask: What happened three years after 1927 on July 4? George Washington's face was dedicated.

In what year did that happen? 1930 (Note: if students are not ready to do the necessary math, you should complete the addition for them.)

How were you able to figure that out? by adding 3 to 1927

Write *July 4, 1930* and what happened on that date on an index card.

Open and fold back the page to see **3** .

Explore "Marvelous Mount Rushmore"
Facts for Four Presidents

1. Cut out the pictures.
2. Glue the pictures in the correct places on Mount Rushmore on page LC 185.
3. Write a fact about each president.

LITERATURE & COMPREHENSION

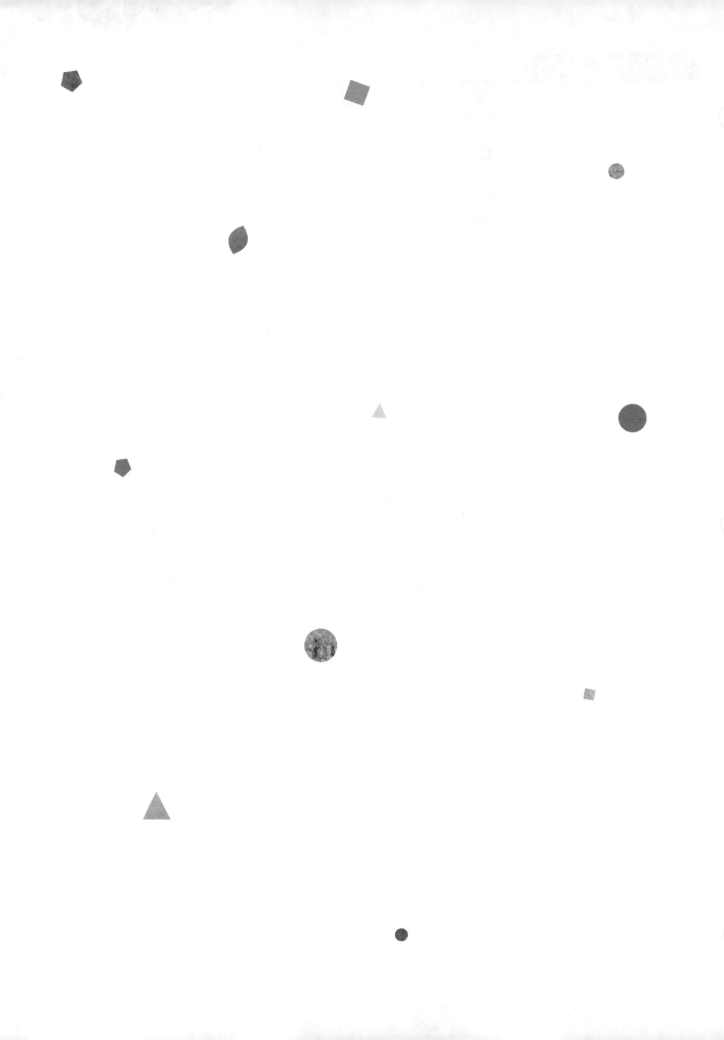

Glue the pictures in the correct places on Mount Rushmore.
Write a fact about each president.

Fact

Fact

Fact

Fact

Introduce "George Washington: American Hero"

Periods

Read aloud the paragraph **without periods**. Then, turn the page over and read aloud the paragraph **with periods**.

George Washington was born in 1732 He was born in the English colony of Virginia His father owned a lot of land there George grew up on his father's land, or plantation

George Washington was born in 1732. He was born in the English colony of Virginia. His father owned a lot of land there. George grew up on his father's land, or plantation.

Introduce "George Washington: American Hero"

Periods

Fold the page into thirds so that the section labeled ① is showing. Use an accordion, or Z, fold (see the diagram). Use this Reading Aid to read "George Washington: American Hero" with students.

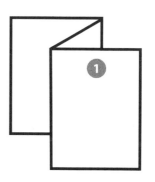

You will read two versions of the first paragraph of "George Washington: American Hero" to students to demonstrate the effect of punctuation. Follow the instructions below.

Tell students that while the words in a text are important, there are also other marks on the page that help us understand what we're reading.

Hold page LC 187 of K¹² Language Arts *Activity Book* so students can follow along as you read.

Read aloud the passage without pausing for periods. Read in an exaggerated, rushed voice to illustrate how difficult it is to understand the passage without pauses.

Ask: What did you notice about how I read? Guide students to recognize that everything in the passage ran together so it was hard to understand.

What do you think would make this passage easier to read? Guide students to recognize that it would be easier to understand if you took little breaths, or pauses, so they could hear separate ideas.

Flip over to see ②.

①

3

Hold up your hand with palm facing outward to show students a signal that means *stop*.

Reread the passage, pausing at each period and signaling *stop* with your hand.

Tell students that you are going to reread the first few pages of "George Washington: American Hero." You will show where the writer wants readers to pause by holding up your hand for each period. Encourage students to chime in and read aloud with you. When they see a period, they should take a brief pause and hold up a hand to signal *stop*.

Read aloud pages 41–45 of "George Washington: American Hero." Hold up your hand to signal *stop* at each period. Have students do the same.

Ask: Why do writers use periods? to let readers know when to make a brief stop while they're reading

How do periods help us understand what we're reading? Possible answers: Periods keep all the ideas from running together; periods make it easier to hear separate ideas.

2

Turn to page LC 188 in *K¹² Language Arts Activity Book.*

Tell students that you will now read the same passage in a different way.

Tell students to listen closely so they can hear the difference.

Read aloud the passage in a more natural way, pausing at the periods.

Ask: What did you notice this time when I read the passage? Guide students to recognize that the pauses make it easier to understand.

How do you think I knew where to stop briefly, or pause, as I was reading? the dots; the periods

Tell students that a dot at the end of a sentence is called a *period*.

- A period is the signal a writer uses to let readers know when to make a little pause.

- A period helps us understand what we're reading because it separates the different ideas in a passage.

Explain that a period is a little bit like a stop sign. When we see a period, we know that we need to stop briefly.

Open and fold back the page to see **3**.

Introduce "George Washington: American Hero"

Create a Time Line

Cut out the fact boxes. On page LC 193, glue the events in the order that they happened.

1789 George becomes the first American president.	**1799** George dies.	**1752** George inherits Mount Vernon.
1759 George marries Martha.	**1732** George is born in the English colony of Virginia.	

Glue the events from page LC 191 in the order that they happened.

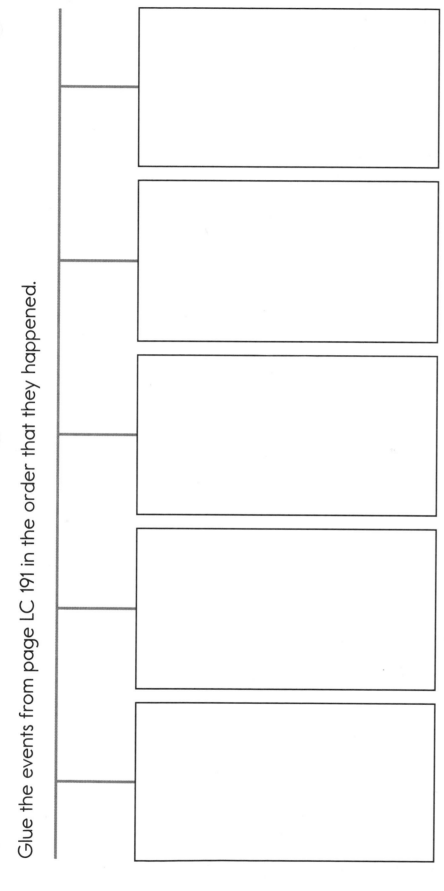

Explore "George Washington: American Hero"
I, George Washington

Complete the facts. Next, cut out the mask on page LC 197, and put it on. Then, use the facts to give a speech.

1. My name is George Washington. I was born

   in the _____ colony in 1732.

2. I like to ride _____ .

3. I have many brothers and _____ .

4. My brother, _____ , helped me get

   my first job as a _____ .

5. My wife's name is _____ .

6. I was the top American _____ in

   the war against _____ .

7. I became the first _____ of the
   United States in 1789.

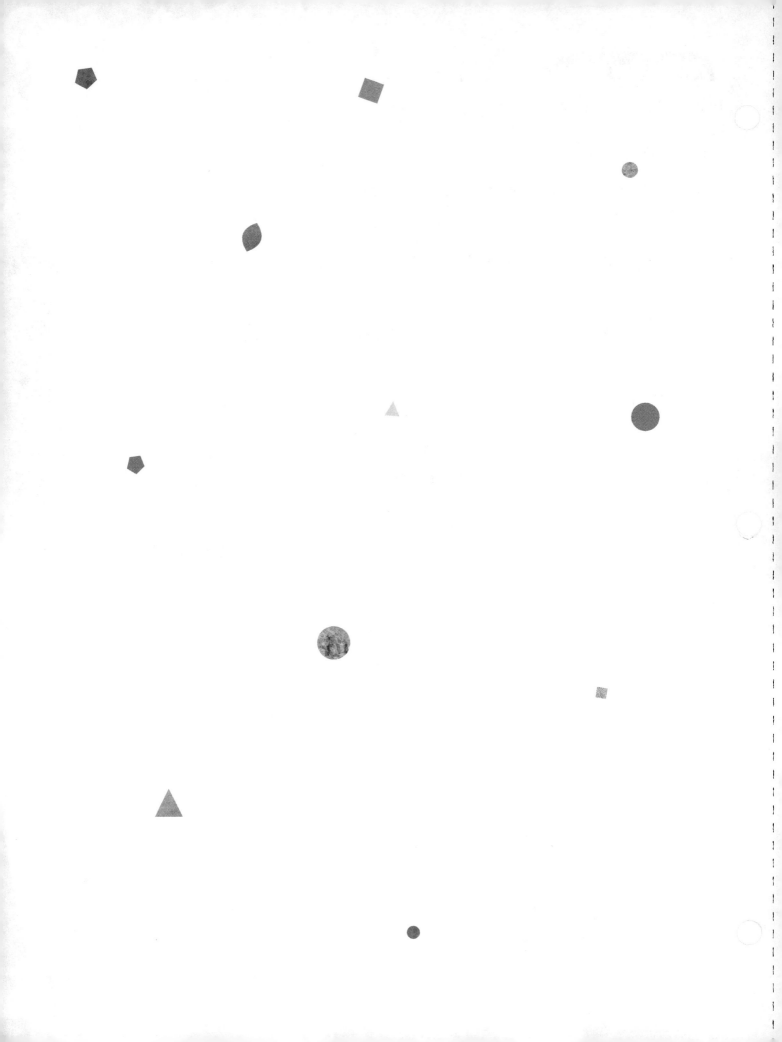

Cut out the mask.

Explore "Washington"
Imagery and Sensory Language

Fold the page into thirds so that the section labeled ① is showing. Use an accordion, or Z, fold (see the diagram). Use this Reading Aid to read "Washington" with students.

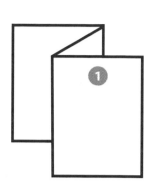

You will read "Washington" with students. Stop at the points indicated and follow the instructions. Answers to questions may vary.

Read aloud the first stanza.

Ask: What did you imagine as you listened to that stanza?

STOP **Have students reread** lines 1–3 of the first stanza as they track with their finger.

Ask: What do you visualize when you hear these lines?

Explain that the poet probably used the action words *raced, fished, climbed,* and *swung* to help readers imagine what Washington was like as a young boy.

STOP **Have students reread** lines 4–6 of the first stanza as they track with their finger.

Ask: Did you hear any words that help you imagine sounds? Possible answers: *hooted; bugles blew*

What do you imagine when you hear the word *hooted*? the sound a bird might make

Flip over to see ②.

①

2

What do you think it would sound like if "one morning, the bugles blew"?

STOP Have students close their eyes as they listen to you read the next stanza. Tell them to try to imagine pictures in their head as they listen to the words.

Read aloud the second stanza.

Ask: What did you imagine as you listened to that stanza?

What did you see when you heard the lines "Over the hills the summons came, / Over the river's shining rim"?

Explain that the poet probably used the phrases *over the hills* and *the river's shining rim* to help readers visualize an outdoor scene of hills and a river with the sun shining on the water.

Read aloud the third stanza.

Ask: What did you imagine as you listened to that stanza?

What did you visualize when you heard the line "Perhaps when the marches were hot and long"?

Open and fold back the page to see **3**.

3

Say: When I hear that line, I imagine soldiers marching with the sun shining down on them. I can imagine that they're feeling really hot and dirty because the sun is hot, they're carrying all their gear, and they're kicking up dirt as they march.

Remind students that the poet carefully chose the words of the poem to help readers see, hear, and feel the events of the poem.

STOP Have students close their eyes as they listen to you reread lines 2–4 of the third stanza. Tell them to try to imagine pictures in their head as they listen to the words.

Ask: What did you imagine as you listened to those lines?

Explain that the poet tells us that "when the marches were hot and long," Washington might have thought of the "river flowing by." What do you think a river flowing by would feel like to someone, especially if it were very hot out? Possible answers: cool; refreshing

What do you think it would look and feel like if you were "camping under a winter sky"? Students may say that it would look very dark with lots of stars shining, and it might feel cold because it's winter.

Open and fold back the page to see **4**.

4

Conclude by sharing with students your favorite word or phrase from the poem and what it makes you see, hear, or feel. For example, you might like the phrase *the whippoorwill's far-off song* because it makes you hear the sound of a singing bird off in the distance.

Ask: Which word or phrase in the poem is your favorite?

Why is that word or phrase your favorite? Does it help you imagine that you can see, hear, or feel something?

Explore "Washington"
Two Washingtons

Complete the graphic organizer.

	"Washington"	**"George Washington: American Hero"**
Type of text		
Has rhyming words		
Gives dates of events		
Tells facts about Washington's family		
Tells things that Washington believed		

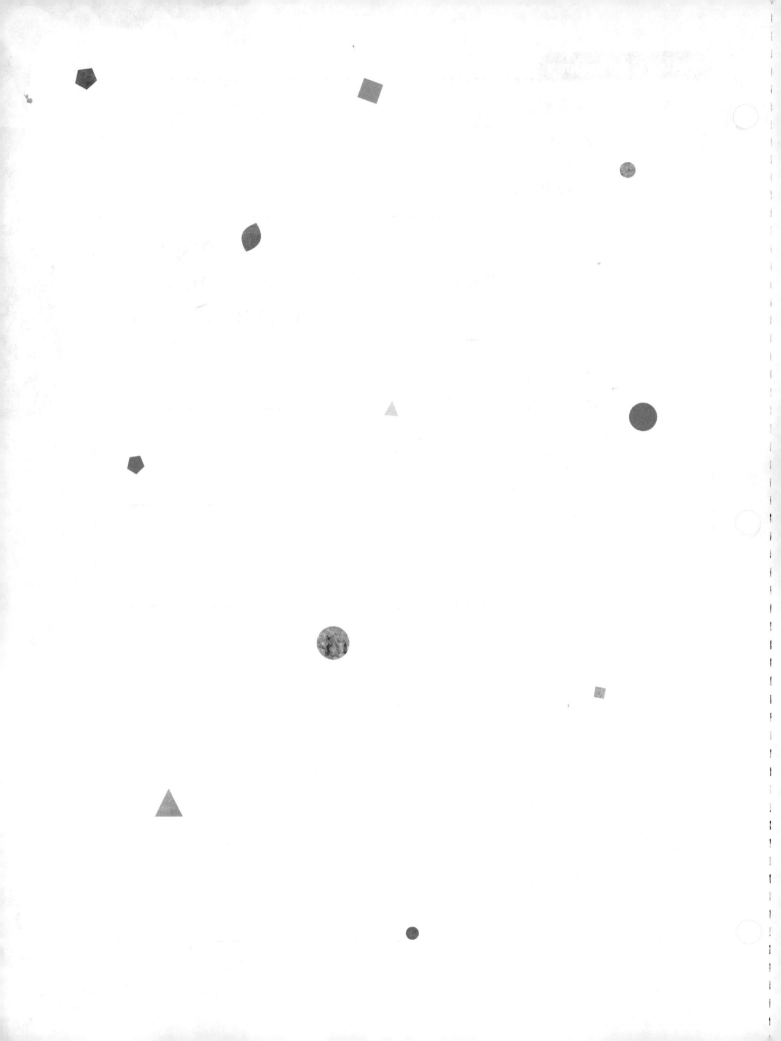

Introduce "Women of the White House"
Words That Indicate a Numbered Order

Fold the page into thirds so that the section labeled ❶ is showing. Use an accordion, or Z, fold (see the diagram). Use this Reading Aid to read "Women of the White House" with students.

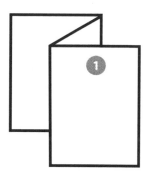

❶

You will read "Women of the White House" with students. Stop at the points indicated and follow the instructions.

Read aloud page 53.

Ask: If we were going to line up all the women who have been First Lady of the United States, who would be first in that line? Martha Washington

Read aloud pages 54 and 55.

Ask: If we were going to line up all the men who have been president of the United States, who would be in the number two position? John Adams   What word do we use to refer to the number two position? *second*

Who would be in the number six position if we were to line up all the men who have been president of the United States? John Quincy Adams   What word do we use to refer to the number six position? *sixth*   How many presidents were there before John Quincy Adams? five

Flip over to see ❷.

4

Check students' ability to place ordinal numbers in the correct order. Mix up the index cards on which you've written the ordinal numbers *first* through *tenth*. Have students arrange the index cards in the correct order. Have them check that they have the correct order by reading the ordinal numbers aloud.

3

With students, read aloud pages 58–61.

Check that students are tracking with their finger as they read and matching their voice to the print.

Explain that the article does not tell us in which position Eleanor Roosevelt would be in our line of First Ladies. However, it's possible to find that information.

Ask: Do you have some ideas about where we could look to learn in which position Eleanor Roosevelt would be in our line of First Ladies? Possible answers: the Internet; books; an encyclopedia

If students show an interest, help them use reference materials to find out Eleanor Roosevelt's position.

Conclude by asking: What are some examples of words that tell us the order of things, such as the order of items in a line? Students may answer with any ordinal number discussed in the lesson.

How do we a change the spelling of the number *four* if we want to say that something is in the number four position? Possible answers: We change it to *fourth*; we add the letters –*th* to the end.

What word do you think we would use to say that something is in the number seven position? *seventh*

Open and fold back the page to see **4** .

2

Explain that the article does not tell us in which position Abigail Adams would be in our line of First Ladies. However, we can infer that information.

Ask: In which position can we infer Abigail Adams would be in our line of First Ladies? *second* What information did you use to make that inference? Abigail Adams was married to John Adams. Since John Adams was the second president, Abigail must have been the second First Lady.

Read aloud pages 56 and 57.

Ask: Which First Lady would be in position number four in our line of First Ladies? Dolley Madison What word do we use to refer to the number four position? *fourth* How many First Ladies were there before Dolley Madison? three

Tell students that that they will read aloud to the end of the article with you. They should practice reading fluently.

Open and fold back the page to see **3** .

Explore "Women of the White House"

"Women of the White House": Time Order

Fold the page into thirds so that the section labeled ❶ is showing. Use an accordion, or Z, fold (see the diagram). Use this Reading Aid to read of "Women of the White House" with students.

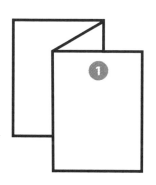

You will read "Women of the White House" with students. Stop at the points indicated and follow the instructions.

Read aloud page 53.

Ask: Did you hear a year mentioned that tells us when an important event happened? 1792   What was the important event? Construction began on the White House.

Explain that there is another clue in the last paragraph on page 53 that can help us figure out when another important event happened.

STOP **Have students reread** the last paragraph on page 53 as they track with their finger.

Ask: What other reference to time did you hear? the phrase *more than 10 years*

Explain that we can add 10 years to the year 1792 to figure out approximately when the White House was completed. (Note: If this math problem is beyond students' ability, you should do the addition.)

Say: If I add 1792 and 10, I get the year 1802. The article says that it took "more than 10 years" to finish the White House. So we know that the White House was finished at some point after 1802.

❶

Flip over to see ❷.

LANGUAGE ARTS GREEN

2

Read aloud pages 54 and 55.

Ask: Did you hear a year mentioned that tells us when an important event happened? 1800   What was the important event? John and Abigail Adams moved into the White House.

The Adamses moved into the White House in 1800. But we figured out that the White House wasn't completed until after 1802. So did the Adams start living in the White House before or after it was finished? before

Read aloud pages 56 and 57.

Ask: Did you hear a year mentioned that tells us when an important event happened? 1814   What was the important event? English soldiers began marching to Washington, D.C.

Did the English soldiers arrive at the White House before or after Dolley Madison left the White House? after   How do you know? What does the article say? It says that Dolley left just in time, and a few hours later the English soldiers arrived. The phrase *a few hours later* means that it happened after Dolley left.

STOP **Have students reread** page 57 as they track with their finger.

Ask: Was the White House rebuilt before or after the war? after

Open and fold back the page to see **3**.

3

Say: Tell me the order in which things happened when Dolley Madison saved objects from the White House. Start with the year 1814 and use words such as *first, next, then,* and *finally.* Possible answer: In 1814, English soldiers marched toward Washington, D.C. First, Dolley chose objects in the White House to save. Next, she had workers pack them in a wagon. Then, she left the White House. Finally, the English soldiers arrived and burned the White House.

Read aloud page 58.

Ask: Did you hear a time period mentioned? the 1930s What was happening during the 1930s? Possible answers: Eleanor Roosevelt was First Lady; many people were poor; people couldn't find jobs.

Explain that when the article says "during the 1930s," that means the years from 1930 to 1939.

Was Eleanor Roosevelt the First Lady before or after Dolley Madison? after   How do you know? Dolley was First Lady in 1814. Eleanor was First Lady in the 1930s. The 1930s came after the year 1814, so Eleanor was First Lady after Dolley.

Open and fold back the page to see **4**.

4

Read aloud page 59.

Ask: Did you hear a year mentioned that tells us when an important event happened? 1939   What was the important event? Marian Anderson gave a concert at the Lincoln Memorial.

Read aloud pages 60 and 61.

Ask: Did you hear a time period mentioned? the 1940s   What was happening during the 1940s? Possible answers: Eleanor Roosevelt was First Lady; the United States was fighting in a big war; Eleanor visited American soldiers.

Conclude by asking: How were we able to figure out the order of important events in this article? the years given in the text; phrases like *10 years after* and *a few hours later*

Explore "Women of the White House"
First Lady Facts

Cut out each First Lady's picture, and glue it next to her name on the shape. Write one fact for each First Lady. Cut out the shape, and fold along the lines. Glue or tape the tabs.

LITERATURE & COMPREHENSION

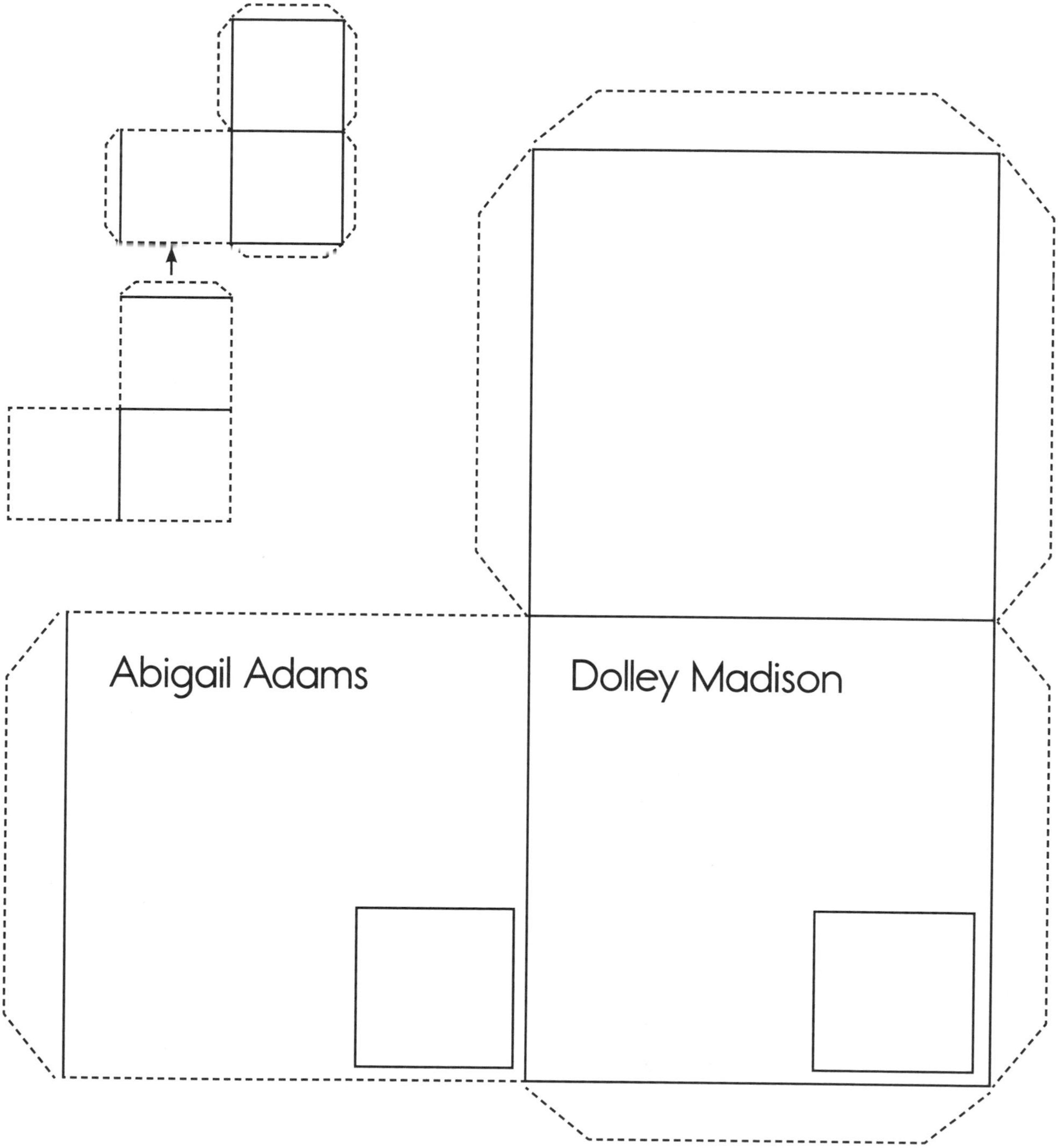

Abigail Adams

Dolley Madison

Martha Washington

Eleanor Roosevelt

Introduce "The Camel and the Pig"

Anticipation Guide for "The Camel and the Pig"

Tell what you believe before you read the story. Check if your ideas change after reading.

What I believe	Before reading	After reading
It's better to be tall.		
It's better to be short.		
It's okay to think you're better than someone else.		
Some people are the best at everything they do.		

Introduce "The Camel and the Pig"

"The Camel and the Pig"

Fold the page into thirds so that the section labeled ❶ is showing. Use an accordion, or Z, fold (see the diagram). Use this Reading Aid to preview the story "The Camel and the Pig" with students.

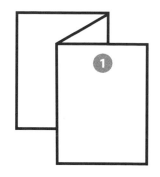

❶

Preview "The Camel and the Pig." Stop at the points indicated and follow the instructions. Answers to questions may vary.

Preview pages 202 and 203.

Ask: Who do you think are the characters in this story? Can you find the words *camel* and *pig* on these pages?

Explain that the camel and pig are both proud because of their height.

Point to the word *proud* in the first paragraph and explain that the *ou* in *proud* makes the sound /ow/.

Point to the word *snout* in the fifth paragraph and explain that this word has the same *ou* spelling pattern as *proud*.

Ask: Knowing that *ou* says /ow/, how would you read this word?

Have students read the word *snout*.

Touch and say the word if students have trouble reading it. Place your finger

- under the letter *s* as you say /s/
- under the letter *n* as you say /n/
- under the letters *ou* as you say /ow/
- under the letter *t* as you say /t/

Flip over to see **❷**.

2

Run your finger under the letters of the word as you say each sound: /s/ /n/ /ow/ /t/. Then blend the sound together to read the word as you run your finger under it.

Ask: What is a snout? Can you point to the pig's snout in the picture? an animal's nose and mouth

What is the camel doing in the picture? eating from a tree

Explain that the tree is in a garden.

Point to the sixth paragraph and have students locate the word *garden*.

Ask: Why do you think the word *garden* is in the story? because that's where things grow that the camel and pig want to eat

Explain to students that they are now going to read aloud the story to you.

As they read, have them stop at certain points so they can make predictions about what will happen next.

Write down all their predictions for later reference.

Open and fold back the page to see **3** .

3

Note: If students have trouble reading on their own, offer one of the following levels of support to meet their needs.

- Read aloud the story to them.
- Read aloud the story as they chime in with you.
- Take turns with students and alternate reading aloud each paragraph.

Remind students to track with their finger as they read.

Have students begin to read aloud page 202.

Have them stop after the pig says that he will give up his snout if he is wrong.

STOP **Ask:** What do you predict will happen next?

Write down all students' predictions for later reference.

Have students read aloud to the end of page 202.

STOP **Ask:** What do you predict will happen next?

Open and fold back the page to see **4** .

4

Have students begin to read aloud page 205.

Have them stop after the camel laughs and asks the pig if he would rather be tall or short.

STOP **Ask:** What do you predict will happen next?

Have students continue to read aloud page 205.

Have them stop after the sentence that says, "the camel was so tall that he could not get through the low gate."

STOP **Ask:** What do you predict will happen next?

Have students read aloud to the end of the story.

Explain that you will refer to students' predictions later in the lesson.

Keep the predictions in a safe place.

Explore "The Camel and the Pig"
Facts and Opinions About Characters

Write facts and opinions to complete the table.

	Camel	Pig
Character's opinion		
Fact about the character		
My opinion of the character		
Fact about this type of animal		

Introduce "Heron and the Hummingbird"
Predict-o-Gram

Read the story words and phrases. Write the words and phrases in the boxes where you predict they belong.

Word Bank

Heron	flowers	flying all night long
river	nectar	owned all the fish
race	sipped nectar	not enough fish
won	Hummingbird	slept all night long

	Story words and phrases
Characters	
Setting	
Problem	
Characters' actions	
Solution	

Introduce "Heron and the Hummingbird"

"Heron and the Hummingbird"

Fold the page into thirds so that the section labeled ❶ is showing. Use an accordion, or Z, fold (see the diagram). Use this Reading Aid to preview the story "Heron and the Hummingbird" with students.

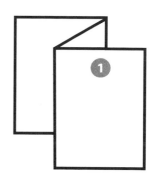

❶

Preview "Heron and the Hummingbird" with students. Stop at the points indicated and follow the instructions. Answers to questions may vary.

Preview pages 206 and 207.

Ask: Who do you think are the characters in this story? Can you find the words *heron* and *hummingbird* on these pages?

Explain that Heron and Hummingbird are very good friends in this story.

Point to the first paragraph and ask: Can you find the word *friends* in this paragraph?

Point to the picture and explain that the story says one of the friends is "tall and gangly and awkward." Which of these birds fits that description? Students should point to the heron.

Explain that the tall bird is Heron.

Point to the bottom of the picture and ask: What do you see swimming in the water? fish

Explain that both birds like to eat fish, but Hummingbird is worried about that. He says, (*track with your finger as you read aloud the quote in paragraph 2 of page 206*) "I am not sure there are enough fish in the world for both of our kind to eat."

Flip over to see ❷.

④

Tell students that they will now read aloud the story to you, but you will give them help if they need it.

Note: If students have trouble reading on their own, offer one of the following levels of support to meet their needs.

- Read aloud the story to them.
- Read aloud the story as they chime in with you.
- Take turns with students and alternate reading aloud each paragraph.

Remind students to track with their finger as they read.

Tell students that, as they read, they should think about the predictions they made in the Predict-o-Gram, and look for the words and phrases from the Predict-o-Gram that describe the story elements.

---

③

Explain that Hummingbird also enjoys the scenery along the way. The word *scenery* is a tough word, so you will show it to them.

Point to the word *scenery* in the first paragraph of page 209.

Preview pages 210 and 211.

Say: Four days is a long time for a race. How do you think Heron and Hummingbird are feeling by the fourth day?

Explain that you will read aloud how Hummingbird feels, because the sentence has some very difficult words in it.

Track with your finger and read aloud the first sentence of paragraph 2 on page 210.

Ask: How do you feel when you wake up in the morning? Do you have a lot of energy?

The story says that Hummingbird feels "refreshed and invigorated." Do you think the hummingbird feels like he has a lot of energy?

Tell students that you don't want to give away the end of the story, but you're wondering if they have an idea of who will win the race.

Open and fold back the page to see **④** .

---

②

Ask: What do you think Heron and Hummingbird will do to solve this problem? have a race

If students do not make this prediction, tell them that the birds decide to have a race.

Ask: Can you find the word *race* at the top of page 207?

Have you ever seen a hummingbird flying? Do they fly quickly or slowly? Which bird do you think is more likely to win the race, the heron or the hummingbird?

Have you ever been in a race? What did you have to do to win the race?

Explain that Heron and Hummingbird decide to race for four days, and the finish line is a dead tree by a river.

Preview pages 208 and 209.

Have students look at the pictures and ask: What do you see Hummingbird doing?

Explain that Hummingbird likes to drink nectar, a sweet liquid, from the flowers. So students will see the word *nectar* many times as they read.

Point to the first paragraph on page 208 and ask: Can you find the word *nectar* in this paragraph?

Open and fold back the page to see **③** .

Introduce "The Tortoise and the Hare"

"The Tortoise and the Hare"

Fold the page into thirds so that the section labeled **1** is showing. Use an accordion, or Z, fold (see the diagram). Use this Reading Aid to preview the story "The Tortoise and the Hare" with students.

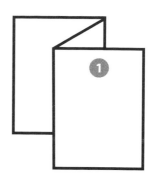

1

Preview "The Tortoise and the Hare" with students. Stop at the points indicated and follow the instructions. Answers to questions may vary.

Preview pages 212 and 213.

Ask: Who do you think are the characters in this story? Can you find the words *tortoise* and *hare* on page 212?

Point to the hare in the picture on page 213.

Ask: What kind of animal is a hare related to? a rabbit

Explain that the hare is a show-off and likes to hop around fast. The hare says, (*track with your finger as you read aloud the quote in the first paragraph*) "Look at me!"

Ask: What kind of punctuation mark do you see at the end of that sentence? an exclamation mark   If it ends with an exclamation mark, how do you think the hare says, "Look at me"? with excitement; in a loud voice   Do you see more exclamation marks on this page 212? Yes

Explain that there are often exclamation marks when the hare speaks, so students should be sure to read with a lot of expression when the hare is talking.

Flip over to see **2**.

④

Have students read aloud page 214.

STOP **Ask:** What do you predict will happen next? Who do you think will win the race?

Have students read aloud to the end of the story.

Explain that you will refer to the students' predictions later in the lesson.

Keep the predictions you wrote down in a safe place.

---

③

Note: If students have trouble reading on their own, offer one of the following levels of support to meet their needs.

- Read aloud the story to them.
- Read aloud the story as they chime in with you.
- Take turns with students and alternate reading aloud each paragraph.

Have students begin to read aloud page 212.

STOP **Have students stop** at the end of the third paragraph on page 212.

Ask: What do you predict will happen next?

Write down all students' predictions for later reference.

Have students read aloud to the end of page 212.

STOP **Ask:** What do you predict will happen next?

Open and fold back the page to see **④** *.*

---

②

Ask: How would you expect a tortoise to move, fast or slow? slow

Explain that the hare says that the tortoise is slow and can only creep.

Point to the third paragraph and ask: Can you find the word *creep* in this paragraph?

Point to the picture on page 213.

Ask: How would you describe where the tortoise and the hare live? Answers will vary.

Explain that the place where the tortoise and the hare live is called a meadow.

Ask: Can you find the word *meadow* in the first paragraph of the story?

Tell students that they will now read aloud the story to you, but you will help them if they need it.

As they read, have them stop at certain points so they can make predictions about what will happen next.

Write down all their predictions for later reference.

Remind students to track with their finger as they read.

Open and fold back the page to see **③** *.*

Explore "The Tortoise and the Hare"
Definition Map: Animal Tales

Answer the question in the box about animal tales.

What is it?	What's it like?

Animal Tale

What are some examples?

LITERATURE & COMPREHENSION

Explore "The Tortoise and the Hare"
Choose a Book Using the 5-Finger Test

1. Pick a book.
2. Choose one page in the book.
3. Read the page. Hold up 1 finger for every word you don't know.
4. If you have 5 fingers up, the book is too hard.
5. Follow the guide to help you choose a book.

**3 Fingers
A little hard**
You may need some
help to read this.

**4 Fingers
Difficult**
You will need
help to read this.

**2 Fingers
Just right**
You can read this
on your own.

**5 Fingers
Too hard**
Save it for
later.

**1 Finger
Easy**
You can
read this
on your own!

5-Finger Rule

Introduce "Come to My House"

"Come to My House"

Fold the page into thirds so that the section labeled ① is showing. Use an accordion, or Z, fold (see the diagram). Use this Reading Aid to preview the story "Come to My House" with students.

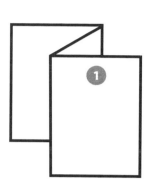

①

Preview "Come to My House" with students. Stop at the points indicated and follow the instructions. Answers to questions may vary.

Preview pages 138 and 139.

Point to the picture of the character holding the toy boat and explain that this character is Rabbit.

Ask: Can you show me the rebus picture that stands for Rabbit in the first line of the story?

Who do you think is the other character in the story? Monkey Can you show me the rebus picture that stands for Monkey somewhere on page 138?

Explain that Rabbit and Monkey are good friends. They want to play together, but they are going to have an argument.

Ask: Do you ever have play dates with friends? Whom do you like to play with?

Have you ever had an argument with a friend? What did you argue about?

Point to the capital letter *U* at the beginning of line 5.

Ask: What letter is this? *U* What word does it stand for? *You*

Flip over to see **②**.

3

Tell students that they will now read aloud the story to you, but you will help them if they need it.

Note: If students have trouble reading on their own, offer one of the following levels of support to meet their needs.

- Read aloud the story to them.
- Read aloud the story as they chime in with you.
- Take turns with students and alternate reading aloud each sentence.

Remind students to track with their finger as they read.

Tell students that as they read, they should think about where the story is happening, what the characters' problem is, and how they solve the problem.

2

Point to line 5 and say: Remember that pictures stand for words in this story. Let's read this line together.

Track with your finger and read aloud line 5 with students. If it is unclear to students, tell them what word each rebus picture stands for.

Point to the pictures of the banana and bread. Explain that these pictures go together to stand for something to eat.

Ask: What do you think it is? banana bread

Preview pages 140 and 141.

Point to the picture of the two telephones together.

Ask: What word do you think these pictures stand for? *telephones*

Why do you think there is more than one picture of a telephone here? because they stand for the word *telephones*, not just one telephone

Point to the picture of Monkey and Rabbit playing at the bottom of page 141.

Ask: Do you think that Monkey and Rabbit are going to work out their problem by the end of the story?

Open and fold back the page to see **3** .

Explore "Come to My House"

Create a Rebus Story

Cut out and glue the pictures to complete the story.

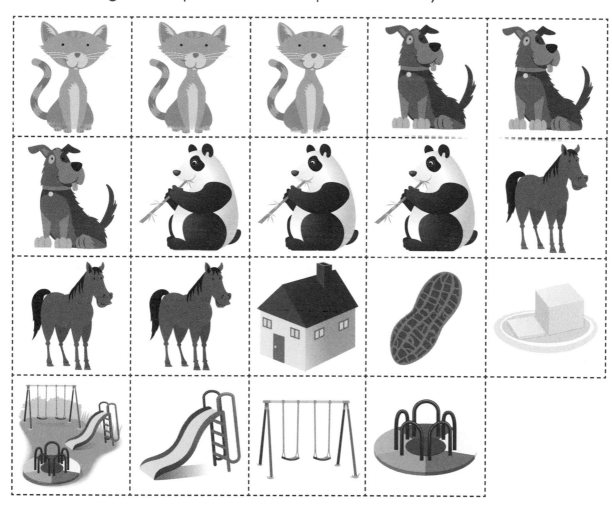

Lunch Buddies

[____] went to [____]'s [____] for lunch. [____] made [____] + [____] and jelly sandwiches. After lunch, [____] and [____] went to the [____] and played on the [____].

Introduce "Ben Franklin, American Inventor"
Predict-o-Gram

Read the article words and phrases. Write the words and phrases in the boxes where you predict they belong.

Word Bank

lawmaker	printer	Philadelphia
bifocals	Boston	Franklin stove
inventor	author	problem solver
hard worker	famous	lightning rod

	Article words and phrases
Places Ben lived	
Ben's jobs	
Ben's inventions	
Words that describe Ben	

Introduce "Ben Franklin, American Inventor"

"Ben Franklin, American Inventor"

Fold the page into thirds so that the section labeled ❶ is showing. Use an accordion, or Z, fold (see the diagram). Use this Reading Aid to preview "Ben Franklin, American Inventor" with students.

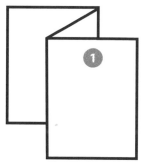

❶

Preview "Ben Franklin, American Inventor" with students. Stop at the points indicated and follow the instructions. Answers to questions may vary.

· ·

Preview pages 2 and 3.

Explain to students that this article is a biography about a man named Ben Franklin who was born in America before the colonies won their independence from England and became the United States.

Ask: This is a biography, so what kind of information about Ben Franklin do you think you will find in the article? Possible answers: when he was born; where he lived; things about his family; important things he did

Part of the article's title is "American Inventor." What do you think an inventor does?

Point to and read aloud the first sentence of the article.

Explain to students that Ben Franklin was born in 1706, which was more than 300 years ago, but some of his inventions are still used today.

Ask: Can you find the word *invention* near the bottom of page 3?

Flip over to see ❷.

2

Preview pages 4 and 5.

Explain to students that during Ben's time, a boy often started learning a job when he was young. When Ben was only 12, he started learning to be a printer from his brother.

Ask: Can you find the word *printer* in the first paragraph of page 4?

Explain that Ben moved to a city called Philadelphia, which was in the Pennsylvania colony.

STOP The words *Philadelphia* and *Pennsylvania* are very hard to read, so show them to students.

Point to and read aloud the words *Philadelphia, Pennsylvania,* in paragraph 2 on page 4.

Explain that Ben printed other people's books, but he also wrote his own book, *Poor Richard's Almanac*. Almanacs are published every year. During Ben's time, an almanac was an important reference for farmers because it gave weather predictions for the whole year. Ben's almanacs were very popular because he included wise sayings, such as the saying at the end of paragraph 2 on page 5.

Point to and read aloud "Lost time is never found again." Explain that this means that time is valuable and should not be wasted.

Open and fold back the page to see **3**.

3

Preview pages 6 and 7.

Explain that the next pages of the article focus on some of Ben's inventions.

Point to the picture on page 6 and ask: What is this? a fireplace   Can you find the word *fireplaces* on this page?

Explain that these big, open fireplaces often caused fires, which was a problem that Ben wanted to solve.

Preview pages 8 and 9.

Explain that lightning set many houses on fire, another problem that Ben wanted to solve.

Ask: Can you find the word *lightning* on page 8?

Preview pages 10 and 11.

Point to the picture of the bifocals at the top of page 10.

Explain that Ben invented a special kind of eyeglasses. Can you find the word *eyeglasses* in the first paragraph of page 10?

Explain that these special eyeglasses are called bifocals, which many people use even today.

STOP The word *bifocals* is a tough word, so show it to students.

Point to and read aloud the word *bifocals* in the first paragraph of page 10.

Open and fold back the page to see **4**.

4

Preview pages 12 and 13.

Explain that these pages focus on the later part of Ben's life and tell us why he is called a founding father of the United States.

Tell students that they will now read aloud the article to you, and you are there if they need your help.

Note: If students have trouble reading on their own, offer one of the following levels of support to meet their needs.

- Read aloud the article to them.
- Read aloud the article as they chime in with you.
- Take turns with students and alternate reading aloud each paragraph.

Remind students to track with their finger as they read.

Tell students that as they read, they should look for the words and phrases from the Predict-o-Gram and think about the predictions they made about those words and phrases.

Explore "Ben Franklin, American Inventor"

How Ben Franklin Solved Problems

Draw a line from each problem to its solution.

Problem	Solution

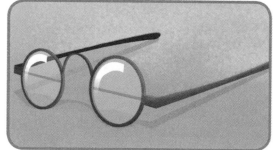

LITERATURE & COMPREHENSION

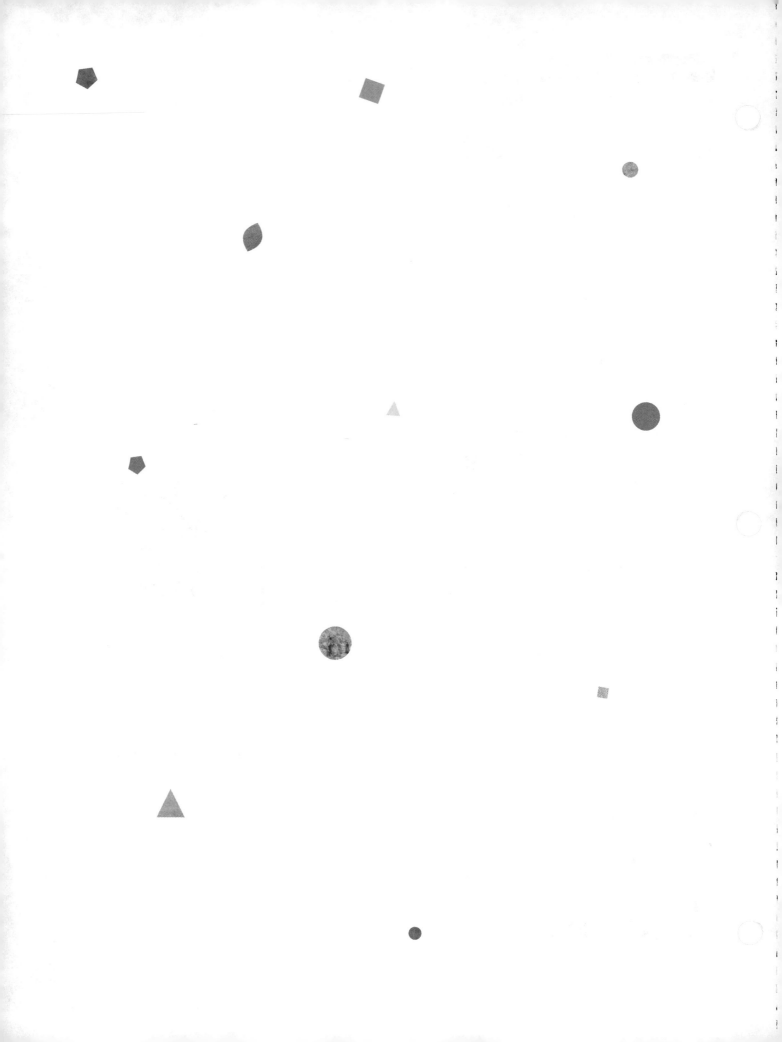

Introduce "Inventors in the Kitchen"

Anticipation Guide for "Inventors in the Kitchen"

Tell what you believe before you read the article. Check if your ideas change after reading.

What I believe	Before reading	After reading
My life is easier than the life of someone who lived before we had microwave ovens and frozen foods.		
Paper bags have always had flat bottoms.		
An inventor came up with the idea for freezing food after seeing how quickly fish froze in the winter.		

LITERATURE & COMPREHENSION

What I believe	Before reading	After reading
People have always had some kind of machine to help them wash dishes.		
In the past, people had to use blocks of ice to keep food cold.		
My life is better because of inventors' ideas and hard work.		

Introduce "Inventors in the Kitchen"

"Inventors in the Kitchen"

Fold the page into thirds so that the section labeled ① is showing. Use an accordion, or Z, fold (see the diagram). Use this Reading Aid to preview "Inventors in the Kitchen" with students.

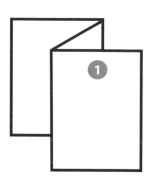

①

Preview "Inventors in the Kitchen" with students. Stop at the points indicated and follow the instructions. Answers to questions may vary.

Preview pages 14 and 15.

Explain to students that this article is a biography about five inventors.

Ask: This is a biography, so what kind of information about these inventors do you think you will find in the article? Possible answers: when they were born; what they invented; where they lived; when they died

Based on the title of the article, where do you think we can find the inventions that the article will tell us about? in the kitchen

The article is about inventions and inventors. Can you find the word *inventions* on page 14? Can you find the word *inventors* on page 14?

Preview pages 16 and 17.

Explain to students that these pages are about a woman named Margaret Knight. Point to and read aloud her name on page 16.

Tell students that Margaret Knight invented a very important machine. They will see the word *machine* in this part of the article and in other sections.

Ask: Can you find the word *machine* in the last paragraph on page 17?

Flip over to see ②.

2

Preview pages 18 and 19.

Ask: Have you ever seen frozen foods in the grocery store made by a company called Birds Eye®?

Explain that the company is named for Clarence Birdseye, whom they will read about in this section of the article. We can thank Clarence Birdseye for the food that we find in the freezer section of the grocery store. Clarence got the idea for freezing food when he spent time in northern Canada with the Inuit people.

Point to and read aloud the word *Inuit* on page 18. *Inuit* is pronounced IH-noo-wuht.

Explain that the frozen food we buy in the grocery store is prepared and frozen in factories.

Ask: Can you find the word *factories* in the last paragraph on page 19?

Preview pages 20 and 21.

Point to the color picture on page 21 of the man in warm clothes loading the truck.

Ask: Why do you think this man is dressed in these clothes while he loads the truck? Possible answers: to stay warm; because he's loading cold things

Open and fold back the page to see ③.

3

Explain that this section is about Frederick McKinley Jones, the man who made it possible for trucks to carry cold items, because he invented a new kind of refrigerator.

Ask: Can you find the word *refrigerators* on page 20?

Preview pages 22 and 23.

Ask: When was the last time you had popcorn that was popped in a microwave?

Explain that a man named Percy Spencer discovered something by accident. Thanks to this accident, we now have microwave ovens, which are used to cook all sorts of food, including popcorn.

Preview pages 24 and 25.

Point to and read aloud the name *Josephine Cochrane* on page 24. *Cochrane* is pronounced KAHK-ruhn.

Ask: What do you think Josephine Cochrane invented? the dishwasher

Explain that the first dishwashers were sold to restaurants.

Ask: Why do you think somebody who runs a restaurant would want a machine that washes dishes? because restaurants use a lot of dishes

Can you find the word *restaurants* in the last paragraph on page 25?

Open and fold back the page to see ④.

4

Tell students that they will now read aloud the article to you, but you are there if they need help.

Note: If students have trouble reading on their own, offer one of the following levels of support to meet their needs.

- Read aloud the article to them.
- Read aloud the article as they chime in with you.
- Take turns with students and alternate reading aloud each paragraph or page.

Remind students to track with their finger as they read.

Tell students that as they read, they should try to figure out the big idea, or important message, of the article.

Explore "Inventors in the Kitchen"
What Would You Invent?

Write a problem you would like to solve, and then draw a picture of what you would invent to solve it. Write the name of your invention below the picture.

Problem _____

_____

Name of invention _____

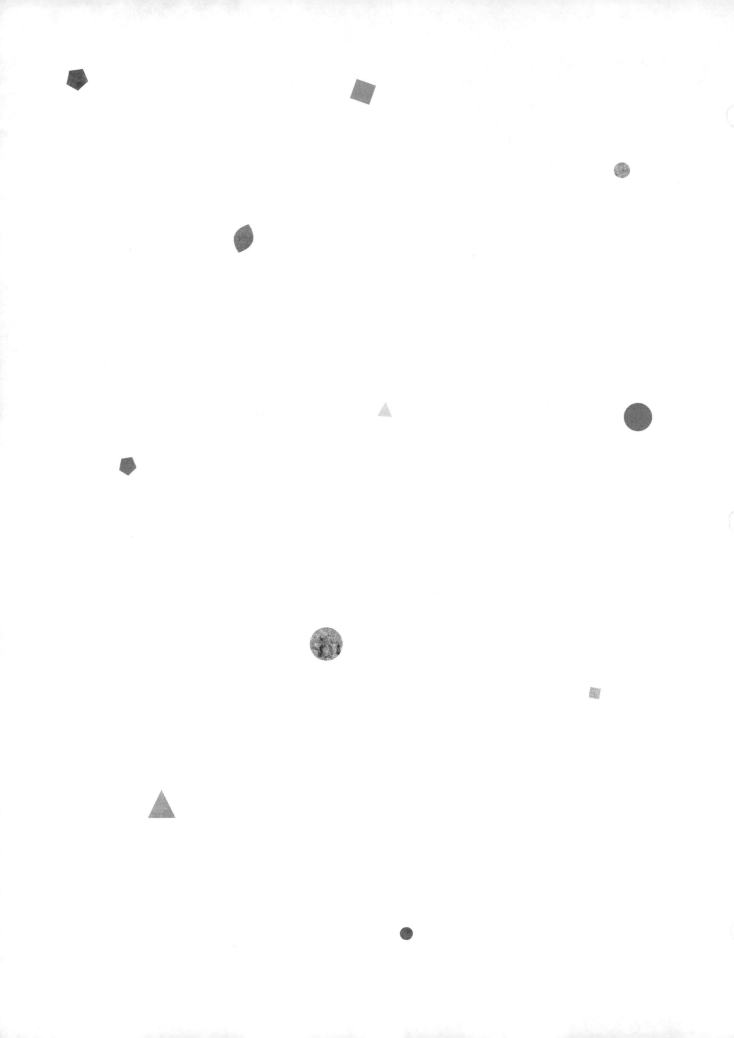

Introduce "Robert's Rockets"
"Robert's Rockets"

Fold the page into thirds so that the section labeled
1 is showing. Use an accordion, or Z, fold (see the
diagram). Use this Reading Aid to preview "Robert's
Rockets" with students.

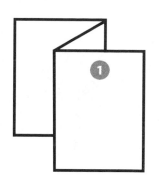

1

Preview "Robert's Rockets" with students.
Stop at the points indicated and follow the
instructions. Answers to questions may vary.

Preview pages 28 and 29.

Explain to students that this article is a biography
about a man named Robert H. Goddard, whose
inventions made it possible for people to travel
in outer space and to the moon.

Ask: This is a biography, so what kind of
information about Robert H. Goddard do
you think you will find in the article? Possible
answers: when he was born; where he lived;
things about his family; important things he did

Explain to students that inventors' discoveries and
inventions happen because they first have an idea.
The word *idea* is in this article many times and is
probably found in any text about an inventor.

Ask: Can you find the word *idea* in the last
paragraph on page 29?

Explain to students that Robert H. Goddard's
goal was space travel, so the word *space* is also in
this article many times.

Ask: Can you find the word *space* in the last
paragraph on page 29?

Preview pages 30 and 31.

Tell students that Robert first began his
experiments with rockets when he was in college
and that Robert studied math and science in college.

Flip over to see **2***.*

2

Ask: Can you find the word *science* in the first line on page 30?

Point to the year 1907 in paragraph 2 on page 30.

Say: I see the year 1907 here in the text. That's a clue to how the author organized the information in this article. I think that the information is organized in the order that the events happened.

Ask: Do you remember what it's called when a text is organized according to the order in which things happened? Possible answers: in sequence; in chronological order

Explain to students that they may come across some long words in this article. One strategy for figuring out those words is to look for a smaller word that they recognize within the big word.

Point to the word *newspaper* on page 31 and help students decode the word.

Ask: Do you see any words within this long word that you recognize?

If students have trouble picking out the words *news* and *paper*, help them by covering up the word *paper* with your finger so that only the word *news* is visible. Then do the same and cover the word *news*.

Open and fold back the page to see **3**.

© K12 Inc. All rights reserved.

3

Preview pages 32 and 33.

Explain that these pages talk about Robert's tests with a new kind of fuel for making his rockets fly. Remind students that fuel provides the power to make things go. For example, we must eat food because it is the fuel that our bodies need to go, and gasoline is the fuel that makes cars go.

Point to and read aloud the words *liquid* and *gasoline* on page 32. Tell students that they can understand what a liquid is if they think about water. Water is a liquid.

Explain that gasoline is a liquid, and that's what Robert used to make a new kind of fuel for his rockets.

Preview pages 34 and 35.

Explain that these pages talk about how Robert tested his rockets and then made changes to improve them. He never gave up if a rocket didn't work.

Preview pages 36 and 37.

Explain that these pages talk about the United States space program and how important Robert's ideas were for making that program happen. Robert's ideas made it possible for astronauts to fly in space and to the moon.

Ask: Can you find the word *astronauts* in the last paragraph on page 36?

Open and fold back the page to see **4**.

4

Point to the time line on page 37.

Ask: What is this text feature called? a time line   Because this article is a biography about Robert H. Goddard, what information do you think is in this time line? important events in Robert's life

Tell students that they will now read aloud the article to you, and you are there if they need help.

Note: If students have trouble reading on their own, offer one of the following levels of support to meet their needs.

- Read aloud the article to them.
- Read aloud the article as they chime in with you.
- Take turns with students and alternate reading aloud each paragraph or page.

Remind students to track with their finger as they read.

Tell students that as they read, they should look for important dates and events in Robert H. Goddard's life.

Explore "Robert's Rockets"

Sequence Events in "Robert's Rockets"

Cut out the fact boxes. On page LC 251, glue the facts in the order that they happened.

Today
Robert is called the "father of rocket science."

1907
Robert sets off a rocket in a basement.

1958
The United States starts a space program.

1899
Robert has an idea in a cherry tree.

1926
Robert makes a new rocket that uses liquid fuel.

Glue the facts from page LC 249 in the order that they happened.

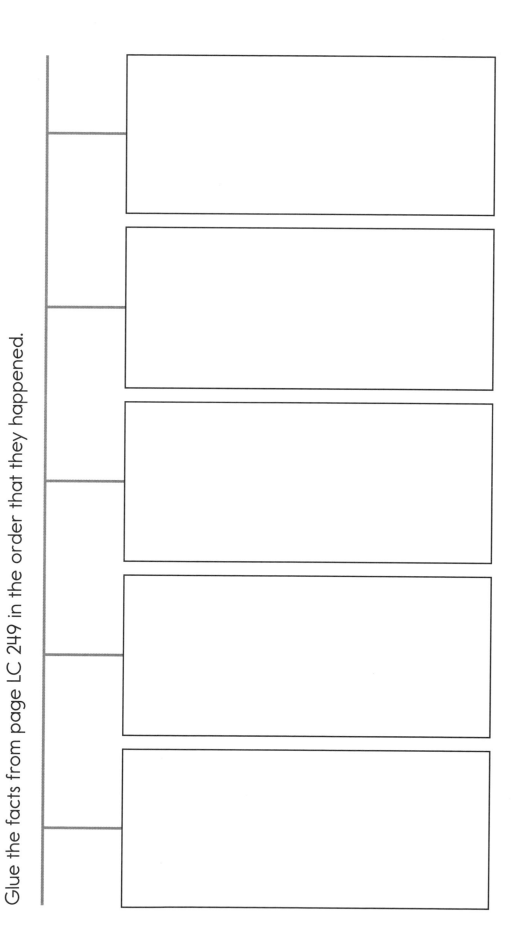

Introduce "Stephanie Kwolek's Amazing Invention"

"Stephanie Kwolek's Amazing Invention"

Fold the page into thirds so that the section labeled **1** is showing. Use an accordion, or Z, fold (see the diagram). Use this Reading Aid to preview "Stephanie Kwolek's Amazing Invention" with students.

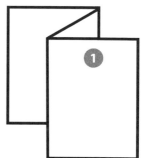

1

Preview "Stephanie Kwolek's Amazing Invention" with students. Stop at the points indicated and follow the instructions. Answers to questions may vary.

Preview pages 38 and 39.

Explain to students that this article is a biography about an inventor named Stephanie Kwolek.

Ask: This is a biography, so what kind of information about Stephanie Kwolek do you think you will find in the article? Possible answers: when she was born; where she lived; things about her family; important things she did

Explain to students that when Stephanie was young, it was unusual for women to study science. But science was one of Stephanie's best subjects in school.

Ask: Can you find the word *science* in the last paragraph of page 38?

A person who works in science is called a scientist. Can you find the word *scientist* in the last paragraph of page 38?

Preview pages 40 and 41.

Ask: The heading for this part of the article is "School and Work." What do you think these pages will talk about? Possible answers: what Stephanie studied in school; where she went to school; what kind of job she got after school; where she worked

Flip over to see **2**.

2

Tell students that Stephanie wanted to be a doctor.

Ask: Can you find the word *doctor* in the first paragraph of page 40?

Explain to students that a person must go to medical school to become a doctor.

Point to and read aloud the words *medical school* on page 40.

Tell students that Stephanie got a job for a company called DuPont in Buffalo, New York.

Point to and read aloud the words *DuPont* and *Buffalo, New York*, on page 41.

Ask: Why do these words begin with capital letters? because they are the names of a company, a city, and a state; because names start with capital letters

Preview pages 42 and 43.

Point to and read aloud the word *fibers* in the heading on page 42.

Explain to students that Stephanie's job at DuPont was to make new kinds of fibers. Another word for fiber is *thread*. Our clothes are made of fibers, or threads, and if we look closely, we can see how the fibers in our clothes are woven together.

Open and fold back the page to see **3** .

3

Preview pages 44 and 45.

Explain to students that Stephanie made different liquids to turn into fibers. If students don't remember what a liquid is, remind them that water and milk are liquids.

Ask: Can you find the word *liquid* on page 44?

Explain to students that Stephanie discovered a new fiber that DuPont named Kevlar®.

Tell students that as they read, they should look for reasons that Kevlar is so special.

Preview pages 46 and 47.

STOP **Have students point to and read aloud** the heading on page 46, and look at the pictures on pages 46 and 47.

Ask: What do you think this section is about? Possible answers: how Kevlar has saved people; things that are made of Kevlar

Explain to students that police officers often wear vests made of Kevlar.

Ask: Can you find the word *police* in the first paragraph on page 46?

Point to and read aloud the words *Seattle, Washington*, on page 46. Explain that Seattle was one of the first cities where police officers wore Kevlar vests.

Open and fold back the page to see **4** .

4

Preview pages 48 and 49.

Explain to students that Kevlar is used in many things. This section will tell a few of those items.

Tell students that they will now read aloud the article to you, and you are there if they need help.

Note: If students have trouble reading on their own, offer one of the following levels of support to meet their needs.

- Read aloud the article to them.
- Read aloud the article as they chime in with you.
- Take turns with students and alternate reading aloud each paragraph or page.

Remind students to track with their finger as they read.

Tell students that, as they read they, should look for important dates and events in the article.

Introduce "Stephanie Kwolek's Amazing Invention"

Create a Time Line

Cut out the fact boxes. On page LC 257, glue the facts in the order that they happened.

1946 Stephanie gets a job at DuPont in Buffalo, New York.	**1975** Police officers in Seattle, Washington, start to use Kevlar vests.
1923 Stephanie is born in New Kensington, Pennsylvania.	**1965** Stephanie tries to make a new fiber to improve car tires.

LITERATURE & COMPREHENSION

Glue the facts from page LC 255 in the order that they happened.

Explore "Stephanie Kwolek's Amazing Invention"

Compare and Contrast Two Inventors

Write the answer for each scientist.

Robert H. Goddard	Biography Fact	Stephanie Kwolek
	When and where born	
	Studied what in college	
	Idea or invention	
	Result of invention	
	Year died	

Explore "My Shadow"

"My Shadow"

Fold the page into thirds so that the section labeled ❶ is showing. Use an accordion, or Z, fold (see the diagram). Use this Reading Aid to preview "My Shadow" with students.

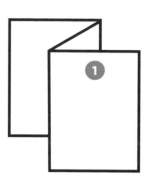

❶

Preview "My Shadow." Stop at the points indicated and follow the instructions. Answers to questions may vary.

·······································

Preview the first stanza.

Point to the picture on page 22.

Ask: The poem is called "My Shadow." Can you show me in this picture which is the shadow?

Can you find the word *shadow* in the first line of the poem?

What do you know about shadows? Do you know what causes them?

Point to and read aloud the third line of the stanza.

Ask: Why do you think the narrator says that his shadow is "very, very like me from the heels up to the head"? because he casts the shadow so it will look like him

Preview the second stanza.

Point to and read aloud the phrase and the definition for *India-rubber ball* at the top of page 23.

Explain that this poetry book puts definitions for unusual words right next to the poems. This term has a definition because we don't call rubber bouncy balls *India-rubber balls* anymore.

Flip over to see ❷.

3

Tell students that they will now read aloud the poem to you, and you are there if they need help.

Note: If students have trouble reading on their own, offer one of the following levels of support to meet their needs.

- Read aloud the poem to them.

- Read aloud the poem as they chime in with you.

- Take turns with students and alternate reading aloud each line or stanza.

Remind students to track with their finger as they read.

Tell students that as they read, they should look for ways that the narrator, or the person telling the story in the poem, makes his shadow sound as if it's a real person.

2

Preview the third stanza.

Explain that you will point out the difficult words in this stanza.

Point to and read aloud the word *notion.* Explain that the part of the word spelled *tion* says /shun/.

Point to and read aloud the word *ought.* Explain that the part of the word spelled *ough* makes the short –*o* sound like in *hot.*

Preview the last stanza.

Explain that sometimes students will come across long words. One way to figure out those words is to look for smaller words that they recognize within the longer word.

Point to the word *buttercup* and help students to decode the word.

Ask: Do you see any small words within this long word that you recognize?

If students have trouble picking out the words *butter* and *cup,* help them by covering up the word *cup* with your finger so that only the word *butter* is visible. Then do the same by covering up the word *butter.*

If students don't know what a buttercup is, explain that it's a small yellow flower.

Open and fold back the page to see **3***.*

Introduce *Who Will Be My Friends?*

What Makes a Good or Bad Friend?

Write your opinions on what makes a good or bad friend.

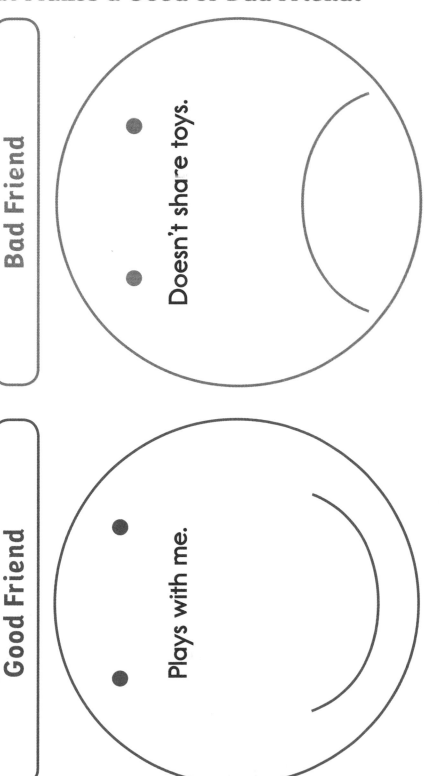

Good Friend

Plays with me.

Bad Friend

Doesn't share toys.

LITERATURE & COMPREHENSION

Introduce *Who Will Be My Friends?*

Who Will Be My Friends?

Fold the page into thirds so that the section labeled ❶ is showing. Use an accordion, or Z, fold (see the diagram). Use this Reading Aid to preview *Who Will Be My Friends?* with students.

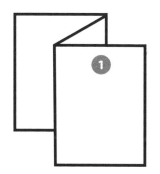

Preview *Who Will Be My Friends?* Stop at the points indicated and follow the instructions. Answers to questions may vary.

Preview page 3.

Ask: Who do you think is a character in this story? Freddy

Point to and read aloud the sentence on page 3.

Preview page 3.

Preview pages 4–7.

Ask: What do you think is happening in the pictures on these pages?

Explain that Freddy is looking for new friends in this story.

Ask: Can you find the word *friends* on page 6?

Have students read aloud the question on page 6.

Tell students that Freddy will ask this question several times in the book.

Point to the quotation marks on page 6.

Ask: What are these called? quotation marks What do quotation marks tell us? that somebody is talking out loud

Flip over to see ❷.

❶

3

Have students read aloud pages 3–9.

STOP **Ask:** What do you predict will happen next?

Write down all students' predictions for later reference.

Have students read aloud pages 10–15.

STOP **Ask:** What do you predict will happen next?

Have students read aloud pages 16–21.

STOP **Ask:** What do you predict will happen next?

Have students read aloud pages 22–29.

STOP **Ask:** What do you predict will happen next?

Have students read aloud to the end of the story.

Explain that you will refer to students' predictions later in the lesson. Keep the predictions in a safe place.

2

Tell students that they will see quotation marks throughout the story, which means that characters will be speaking out loud. So when students read the words inside the quotation marks, they should make it sound like somebody is talking.

Explain that students are going to read aloud the story to you. As they read, you will have them stop at certain points so they can make predictions about what will happen next. You will write down all their predictions for later reference.

Note: If students have trouble reading on their own, offer one of the following levels of support to meet their needs.

- Read aloud the story to them.
- Read aloud the story as they chime in with you.
- Take turns with students and alternate reading aloud each page.

Remind students to track with their finger as they read.

Open and fold back the page to see **3** *.*

Explore *Frog and Toad Are Friends* (A)
"Spring" and "The Story"

Fold the page into thirds so that the section labeled
1 is showing. Use an accordion, or Z, fold (see the
diagram). Use this Reading Aid to preview "Spring" and
"The Story" with students.

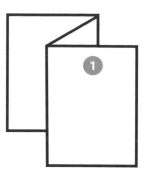

1

Preview "Spring" and "The Story" in *Frog
and Toad Are Friends.* Stop at the points
indicated and follow the instructions.
Answers to questions may vary.
• •

Preview pages 4 and 5.

Ask: Can you find the words *Frog* and *Toad*
on these pages? What do you notice about
how the words are written?

Explain that these are the characters' names,
so they begin with capital letters.

Ask: In the picture, what do you see on
the roof and ground? Have you ever been
somewhere that has snow in the winter?

The story says, "The snow is melting." What
time of year do you think it is?

How do you think people feel when spring
arrives after a long, snowy winter?

Preview pages 6–11.

Explain that Frog is the taller, green
character, while Toad is the shorter,
brown character.

Ask: Where do you think the story is
happening?

Do you think Toad wants to get out of bed?
What do you think Frog is saying to Toad?

Flip over to see **2**.

2

Point to the word *April* on page 8.

Explain that the month of April is in the spring, and Frog is very excited about all the things he and Toad will do outdoors now that spring has arrived.

Ask: What are some things that you like to do outdoors?

Have students scan the text on page 8.

Ask: What are some things that Frog says he and Toad will do?

Preview pages 12–15.

Ask: What is Frog looking at on the wall?

Frog is looking at a calendar. Can you find the word *calendar* on page 12?

Tell students that they will see the names of several months in the story.

Point to and read aloud the names of the months on pages 12 and 13.

Ask: What kind of letter do you see at the beginning of each month? a capital letter

Explain that just like people's names, the name of each month begins with a capital letter.

Open and fold back the page to see ③.

3

Ask: Do you think that Frog will finally convince Toad to get out of bed?

Preview pages 16 and 17.

Explain that at the beginning of "The Story," Frog does not feel well, so Toad says, "Get into my bed and rest."

Ask: What do you do when you don't feel well?

Explain that Frog asks Toad to tell him a story while he's resting.

Preview pages 18–23.

Ask: Do you think that Toad will be able to think of a story to tell Frog?

Explain that Toad has a hard time thinking of a story and does some silly things that he thinks will help him think of one.

Ask: Can you find the sentence "But he could not think of a story to tell Frog" on page 18?

Explain that students will see this sentence repeated several times. Have them read aloud the sentence with you as you track with your finger.

Ask: What are some things that you think Toad will do as he tries to think of a story?

Open and fold back the page to see ④.

4

Preview pages 24–27.

Ask: What is Toad doing on page 24? Do you think that banging his head against the wall will help Toad think of a story?

How do you think Toad feels after he bangs his head against the wall?

Point to the picture on page 27 and ask:

Why do you think Toad is in the bed instead of Frog?

Now Toad is resting instead of Frog. Do you think that Frog will do something for Toad while he's resting?

Tell students that they will now read aloud the stories to you, and you will help them if they need it.

Note: If students have trouble reading on their own, offer one of the following levels of support to meet their needs.

- Read aloud the stories to them.
- Read aloud the stories as they chime in with you.
- Take turns with students and alternate reading aloud each paragraph or page.

Remind students to track with their finger as they read.

Encourage students to think about the following questions as they read.

- When and where are the stories taking place?
- What problems do Frog and Toad have in the stories?

Explore *Frog and Toad Are Friends* (A)

Story Structure Elements in *Frog and Toad Are Friends*

Fill in the chart.

Story title	Setting	Problem	Solution
"Spring"			
"The Story"			

Story title	Setting	Problem	Solution
"A Lost Button"			
"A Swim"			
"The Letter"			

Explore *Frog and Toad Are Friends* (B)
"A Lost Button" and "A Swim"

Fold the page into thirds so that the section labeled ❶ is showing. Use an accordion, or Z, fold (see the diagram). Use this Reading Aid to preview "A Lost Button" and "A Swim" with students.

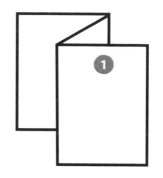

❶

Preview "A Lost Button" and "A Swim" in *Frog and Toad Are Friends.* Stop at the points indicated and follow the instructions. Answers to questions may vary.

Have students read aloud the story title on page 28.

Ask: Have you ever lost something that was important to you? Did you try to find it?

Preview pages 28 and 29.

Explain that Frog and Toad have gone for a long walk.

Ask: Can you find the word *walk* on page 28?

Explain that this is a word that does not sound like it looks. Point to the first occurrence of *walked* and tell students that they will see this form of the word several times in the story. Track with your finger as you read aloud: "They walked across a large meadow. They walked in the woods. They walked along the river."

Ask: Why do you think Toad is looking at his jacket?

Preview pages 30–35.

Ask: Where is this story happening?

What do you think Frog and Toad are doing in this part of the story?

Flip over to see ❷.

2

Have students scan the text on page 31.

Ask: Can you find the sentence that says, "That is not my button,' said Toad"?

Track with your finger as you and students read aloud the sentence. Tell students that they will see this sentence many times in the story.

Preview pages 36–39.

Have students look at the picture on page 36.

Ask: How do you think Toad is feeling? Why might he be feeling that way?

What is Toad doing on page 38?

How do you think Frog and Toad are feeling at the end of the story?

Explain that if students are not sure how to read a word, they can try the following strategy: Look at the first letter of the word, look at the picture, and think about what word would make sense.

Point to the word *buttons* at the top of page 38 and model this strategy.

Open and fold back the page to see **3** *.*

3

Say: I'm not sure what this word is. It starts with the letter *b*. When I look at the picture at the top of this page, I see Toad looking at several buttons. I think that this word is *buttons*.

Preview pages 40 and 41.

Ask: What is the title of the story?

Where are Frog and Toad in the picture on page 41? Where do you think the story is happening?

Tell students that Frog and Toad are going swimming. Toad wears a bathing suit when he swims, but he doesn't like anyone to see him in his bathing suit because he thinks he looks funny.

Ask: Can you find the words *bathing suit* on page 40?

Have students point to and read aloud with you the words *bathing suit*.

Explain that they will see these words many times in the story.

Preview pages 44–49.

Ask: What do you think Frog is saying to the turtle on page 45? What animals will we meet on these pages?

Can you find the names of the animals we see on pages 46 and 47?

Open and fold back the page to see **4** *.*

4

Have students point to and read aloud with you the words *lizards, snake, dragonflies,* and *mouse*.

Preview pages 50–52.

Ask: What is everybody doing in the picture on page 51?

Why do you think they're laughing?

Can you find the word *laughed* on page 51?

How do you think Toad feels when everybody laughs at him?

Tell students that they will now read the stories aloud to you, and you are there to help if they need it.

Note: If students have trouble reading the stories on their own, offer the following levels of support to meet their needs.

- Read aloud the stories to them.
- Read aloud the stories as they chime in with you.
- Take turns with students and alternate reading aloud each paragraph or page.

Remind students to track with their finger as they read.

Encourage students to think about the following questions as they read.

- Why do the characters do the things they do?
- Where are the stories happening?
- What problems do Frog and Toad face in the stories?

Explore *Frog and Toad Are Friends* (B)
Find Toad's Missing Button

Find Toad's button by using the clues that tell what it does **not** look like. Then, complete the sentence.

> It is **not** small.
> It is **not** thin.
> It is **not** square.
> It does **not** have two holes.
> It is **not** red, blue, black, green, or yellow.

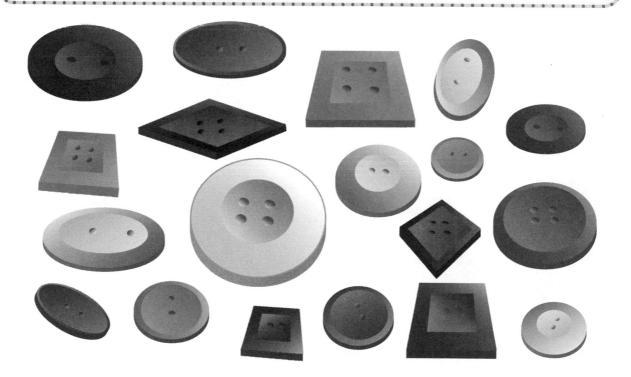

Toad's missing button is _____

_____ .

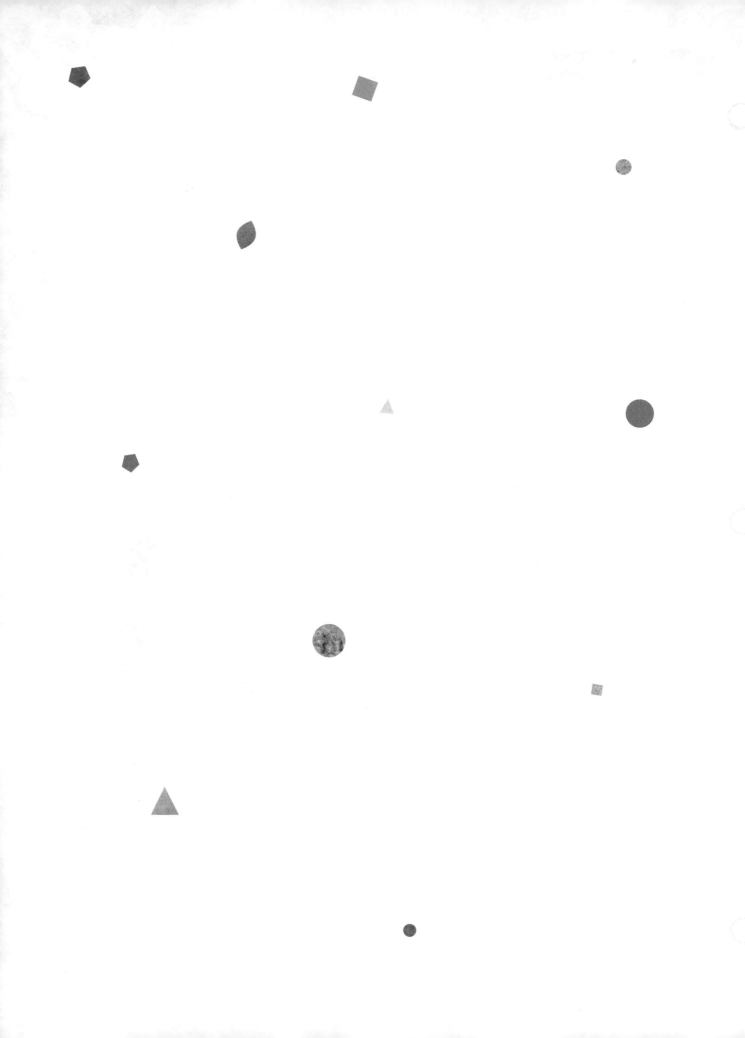

Explore *Frog and Toad Are Friends* (C)
"The Letter"

Fold the page into thirds so that the section labeled **1** is showing. Use an accordion, or Z, fold (see the diagram). Use this Reading Aid to preview "The Letter" with students.

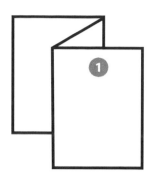

1

Preview "The Letter" in *Frog and Toad Are Friends*. Stop at the points indicated and follow the instructions. Answers to questions may vary.

······································

Have students read aloud the story title on page 53.

Ask: Have you ever received a letter in the mail? Whom was it from? How did you feel when you opened the letter?

Preview pages 53–55.

Have students look at the pictures on pages 53–55.

Ask: How do you think Frog and Toad are feeling?

Explain that if students are not sure how to read a longer word, they can try the following strategy: Look at the word to see if there are any parts of the word or smaller words that they recognize inside the longer word. Then, think about what would make sense in the story.

Point to the word *mailbox* on page 55, and model this strategy.

Say: I'm not sure what this word is, but I see the smaller word *box* is part of the word. I see a picture of a mailbox, and I know the title of the story is "The Letter." We get letters in our mailbox, so I think that this word is *mailbox*.

Flip over to see **2**.

3

Explain to students that they are now going to read aloud the story to you. As they read, you will have them to stop at certain points so they can make predictions about what will happen next. Write down all their predictions for later reference.

Note: If students have trouble reading on their own, offer one of the following levels of support to meet their needs.

- Read aloud the story to them
- Read aloud the story as they chime in with you.
- Take turns with students and alternate reading aloud each page.

Remind students to track with their finger as they read.

Have students read aloud to the middle of page 56.

STOP **Have students stop reading** where the story says, "Frog hurried home."

Ask: What do you think will happen next?

Write down all students' predictions for later reference.

Have students read aloud from the bottom of page 56 to the middle of page 57.

STOP **Have students stop reading** where the story says, "Frog ran out of his house."

Ask: What do you think will happen next?

Have students read aloud to the end of page 63.

Ask: What do you think will happen next?

Have students read aloud to the end of the story.

2

Preview pages 56 and 57.

Have students look at the pictures on pages 56 and 57.

Ask: What do you think Frog is doing?

Have you ever written someone a letter? If so, whom did you write to?

Have students practice the strategy you modeled for reading the word *mailbox*.

Point to the word *pencil* on page 56.

Say: Let's practice figuring out this word. Do you see any part of the word that you recognize? Guide students to see the word part *pen* at the beginning of the word.

Look at the picture on page 56. What do you see Frog doing? Guide students to recognize that Frog is writing something.

Knowing that the word starts with *pen* and seeing that Frog is writing something, what word do you think this is? *pencil*

Preview pages 58–61.

Ask: What do you think Frog is doing on these pages?

Say: I see Frog looking out the window on page 59. Can you find the word *window*?

Open and fold back the page to see **3**.

Explore *Frog and Toad Are Friends* (C)
Tell Me a Story

Cut out the pictures of Frog and Toad. Glue them to craft sticks.
Then, retell your favorite Frog and Toad story with the stick puppets.

Explore *Danny and the Dinosaur* (A)
Pages 5–37

Fold the page into thirds so that the section labeled ❶ is showing. Use an accordion, or Z, fold (see the diagram). Use this Reading Aid to preview pages 5–37 of *Danny and the Dinosaur* with students.

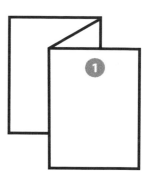

❶

Preview pages 5–37 of *Danny and the Dinosaur.* Stop at the points indicated and follow the instructions. Answers to questions may vary.

Preview pages 5–9.

Point to the picture on page 5.

Ask: Who do you think this character is?
Danny

Explain that Danny is going to the museum and he's going to see many things there.

Tell students that if they come across a word they don't know, they can try this strategy: Look at the first letter of the word, and then look at the picture. Then think about what word would make sense.

Practice the strategy with students. Point to the word *swords* on page 7.

Ask: What letter is at the beginning of this word? s   What do you see in the picture on page 7? swords and guns   Could this word be *swords*? Yes

Point to the word in all capital letters on page 8.

Ask: What word is this? *dinosaurs*   It's written in all capital letters and has an exclamation mark after it, so how should we read this word? in a loud voice; with excitement

2

Preview pages 10–13.

Ask: What do you think is happening in the pictures on these pages?

Point to the quotation marks on page 10.

Ask: What are these called? quotation marks

What do quotation marks tell us? that somebody is talking out loud

Tell students that they will see quotation marks throughout the story, which means that characters will be speaking out loud. So when students read the words inside the quotation marks, they should make it sound like somebody is talking.

Preview pages 14–21.

Ask: Danny and the dinosaur have left the museum. Where do you think they might go?

What kinds of problems do you think a dinosaur might have walking around a city?

Open and fold back the page to see **3** .

3

Point to the pictures on pages 20 and 21.

Explain that there are a lot of buildings in the city.

Ask: Can you find the word *buildings* on page 20?

Preview pages 22–27.

Ask: What are some ways that you think the dinosaur will help people?

How old do you think the dinosaur is?

Explain that the dinosaur gives us a clue about how old he is.

Point to and read aloud what the dinosaur says on page 26.

Preview pages 28–37.

Ask: Where else do you think Danny and the dinosaur will go?

Tell students that they will now read the pages 5–37 aloud to you, but you are there if they need help.

Open and fold back the page to see **4** .

4

Note: If students have trouble reading on their own, offer one of the following levels of support to meet their needs.

- Read the story aloud to them.
- Read the story aloud as they chime in with you.
- Take turns with students and alternate reading each page aloud.

Remind students to track with their finger as they read.

Tell students to think about the question "Who did what?" as they read so that they can give a summary after they finish reading.

LANGUAGE ARTS GREEN

Explore *Danny and the Dinosaur* (B)
Pages 38–64

Fold the page into thirds so that the section labeled
1 is showing. Use an accordion, or Z, fold (see the
diagram). Use this Reading Aid to preview pages 38–64
of *Danny and the Dinosaur* with students.

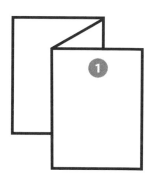

Preview pages 38–64 of *Danny and the Dinosaur*. Stop at the points indicated and follow the instructions. Answers to questions may vary.

Preview pages 38 and 39.

Ask: Why do you think Danny and the dinosaur are leaving the zoo?

Preview pages 40–49.

Point to the pictures on pages 40 and 41.

Explain that these children are Danny's friends.

Ask: Do Danny's friends look like they're scared of the dinosaur? No

How do you think you'd feel if your friend showed up with a real, live dinosaur?

What kinds of things do you think the children and the dinosaur will do together?

Point to the pictures on pages 48 and 49.

Ask: What game are the children playing with the dinosaur? hide-and-seek

What do you think it would be like to play hide-and-seek with a dinosaur?

Flip over to see **2**.

1

❸

Preview pages 60–64.

Ask: Do you think Danny will take the dinosaur home with him?

Do you think you would want to have a dinosaur as a pet? Why or why not?

Tell students that they will now read aloud pages 38 to 64 to you, and you are there if they need help.

Note: If students have trouble reading on their own, offer one of the following levels of support to meet their needs.

- Read aloud the story to them.
- Read aloud the story as they chime in with you.
- Take turns with students and alternate reading aloud each page.

Remind students to track with their finger as they read.

Tell students to think about the question "Who did what?" as they read so that they can give a summary after they finish reading.

---

❷

Preview pages 50–53.

Ask: Whose turn is it to hide? the dinosaur's

Tell students that you are going to practice the strategy for figuring out a word by looking at the first letter of the word and the picture.

Point to the word *sign* on page 53.

Say: Let's try to figure out this word.

Ask: What letter does the word start with? s

Say: I see the dinosaur hiding behind a big sign in the picture.

Ask: What do you think this word is? *sign*

Preview pages 54–59.

Ask: Do you think that the dinosaur will be able to find a place to hide where the children can't find him?

Open and fold back the page to see **❸** .

Explore *Danny and the Dinosaur* (B)
A Good Friend

Complete the sentence. Write what each character would say makes a good friend.

> "A good friend is someone who . . . "

Frog

Toad

"A good friend is someone who . . . "

The Dinosaur

Freddy

Danny

Introduce *A Picture for Harold's Room*
A Picture for Harold's Room

Fold the page into thirds so that the section labeled
1 is showing. Use an accordion, or Z, fold (see the
diagram). Use this Reading Aid to preview *A Picture
for Harold's Room* with students.

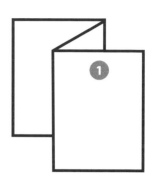

1

Preview *A Picture for Harold's Room* with
students. Stop at the points indicated and
follow the instructions.

....

Preview pages 5–9.

Ask: What's happening in this part
of the story? a little boy is drawing a
picture   Who is the little boy? Harold

Why do you think Harold looks like he's his
usual size in the picture on page 10, but he
looks like he's huge in the picture on page 11?
Answers will vary.

Preview pages 10 and 11.

Ask: What is the difference between the
pictures on these pages? Answers will vary.

Tell students that Harold has stepped into
the picture on page 11. The size of the
houses is the same, but now that Harold is in
the picture and standing next to the houses,
he looks like he's a giant.

Explain to students that sometimes they
will come across a longer word. One strategy
for figuring out that word is to look for a
smaller word that they recognize within the
longer word.

Point to the word *moonlight* on page 10 and
help students decode the word.

Ask: Do you see any words within this
longer word that you recognize?

Flip over to see **2**.

②

If students have trouble picking out the words *moon* and *light*, help them by covering up the word *light* with your finger so that only the word *moon* is visible. Then cover the word *moon* so that only the word *light* is visible.

Preview pages 12 and 13.

Point to and read aloud the word *giant* in capital letters.

Ask: How should we read this word? in a loud voice Why? because it's in all capital letters and there's an exclamation mark

Preview pages 14–19.

Point to the pictures on pages 18 and 19.

Ask: How is Harold changing the straight line he is drawing? He's making it wavy. What is he making the line look like? Possible answers: water; the ocean; the sea

Open and fold back the page to see **③** *.*

③

Preview pages 20–35.

Ask: What are some things that Harold will put in his picture? Possible answers: ships; a whale; a lighthouse; mountains; an airplane

Point to the word *high* on page 30.

Explain that the spelling pattern *–igh* makes the long *i* sound.

Ask: If the letters *igh* say /ī/, what is this word? *high*

Point to the word *highest* on page 31.

Ask: Do you see a word that you recognize in this longer word? *high*

If you know that the first part of this word is *high*, what is the whole word? *highest*

Preview pages 36–47.

Ask: What is Harold drawing on these pages? train tracks; birds; flowers

What do you notice about the size of the things that Harold is drawing? They are getting bigger and bigger.

Open and fold back the page to see **④** *.*

④

What does it look like is happening to Harold's size? It looks like he's shrinking.

Do you think that Harold is really shrinking? Answers will vary.

Tell students that they will now read the book aloud to you, but you are there if they need help.

Note: If students have trouble reading on their own, offer one of the following levels of support to meet their needs.

- Read aloud the story to them.
- Read aloud the story as they chime in with you.
- Take turns with students and alternate reading aloud each page.

Remind students to track with their finger as they read.

Tell students that as they read, they should think about the things that Harold says and does, and what those things tell us about Harold.

Introduce *A Picture for Harold's Room*

Inference Chart

Complete the chart. Then, make an inference about Harold. Draw a picture of Harold in the box.

Facts About Harold	What Harold Says

Harold

What Harold Does	What Harold Thinks or Feels

What I can infer about Harold: _____

_____

Introduce *And I Mean It, Stanley*

And I Mean It, Stanley

Fold the page into thirds so that the section labeled
1 is showing. Use an accordion, or Z, fold (see the
diagram). Use this Reading Aid to preview *And I Mean
It, Stanley* with students.

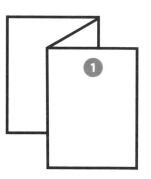

1

Preview *And I Mean It, Stanley* with students.
Stop at the points indicated and follow the
instructions. Answers to questions may vary.
···

**Preview the pictures from the title
page to page 7.**

Ask: Do you think that the character in these
pictures is a boy or a girl? a girl   How can
you tell? She's wearing a skirt.

Why do you think the little girl is looking
under the fence?

Point to the first sentence on page 7
and explain that the little girl is talking to
someone behind the fence, so she says,
"Listen, Stanley," to get Stanley's attention.

Ask: Who do you think is behind the fence?
Stanley   Who do you think Stanley is?

Preview pages 8–11.

Ask: What is the little girl doing in the
pictures on these pages? playing with things
that she finds by the fence

Flip over to see **2**.

2

Point to the last sentence on page 11 and explain that the little girl says, "And I mean it, Stanley," at different times of the story. Tell students that they should think about whether the little girl really means the things she says to Stanley or not.

Preview pages 12–15.

Ask: What is the little girl doing in the pictures on these pages? stacking up the things she found by the fence   Why do you think she's doing that?

Tell students that they will now read aloud the story to you, but you are there if they need help.

As they read, you will have them stop at certain points and ask them to predict who they think Stanley is.

Note: If students have trouble reading on their own, offer one of the following levels of support to meet their needs.

- Read aloud the story to them.
- Read aloud the story as they chime in with you.
- Take turns with students and alternate reading aloud each page.

Open and fold back the page to see **3**.

3

Remind students to track with their finger as they read.

Have students read aloud pages 7–11.

STOP Ask: Who do you think Stanley is?

Have students read aloud pages 12–17.

STOP Ask: Do you think Stanley will come out from behind the fence now?

Who do you think Stanley is?

Have students read aloud pages 18–25.

STOP Ask: Do you think Stanley will come out from behind the fence to see the "really, truly great thing"?

Have you changed your mind about who you think Stanley is?

Have students read aloud pages 26–29.

STOP Ask: Do you think Stanley will come out from behind the fence now?

Have students read aloud to the end of the book.

Explore *Harry and the Lady Next Door* (A)
"The Party" and "Harry's First Try"

Fold the page into thirds so that the section labeled ① is showing. Use an accordion, or Z, fold (see the diagram). Use this Reading Aid to preview "The Party" and "Harry's First Try" in *Harry and the Lady Next Door* with students.

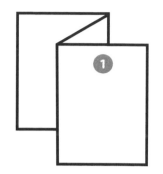

①

Preview "The Party" and "Harry's First Try" with students. Stop at the points indicated and follow the instructions.

Preview the title page.

Ask: This book is called *Harry and the Lady Next Door*. Who do you think this character is? Harry   Why do you think he's looking out the window and growling? Answers will vary.

Preview pages 7–13.

Explain that the lady in the window is Harry's neighbor.

Ask: What is the lady doing? singing Do you think people like her singing? No   How can you tell? People are covering their ears; animals are running away.

Point to the second sentence on page 8 and explain that this sentence tells us about Harry's problem.

Track with your finger and have students read aloud the sentence "She sang high and loud." Explain that the lady's singing hurts Harry's ears.

Point to the word *howled* on page 12 and explain that the spelling pattern *ow* can make two different sounds. In the word *howled* it says /ow/ like in *ouch*. But *ow* can also say /ō/ like in *go*.

Flip over to see ②.

2

Explain that when students see words with *ow*, they will have to decide if it says /ow/ or /ō/.

Tell students that if they come across a word they don't know, they can look at the first letter of the word and look at the picture to figure out what word would make sense.

Practice the strategy with students. Point to the word *piano* at the bottom of page 13.

Ask: What letter is at the beginning of this word? *p* What is the man playing in the picture on page 13? a piano Could this word be *piano*? Yes

Preview pages 14–17.

Point to the picture on pages 14 and 15 and ask: Does it look like these people are happy with Harry? No

Point to the pictures on pages 16 and 17 and explain that the papers in the air are pages of music.

Ask: What is Harry doing with the music pages? running away with them Can you find the word *music* on page 16?

Preview pages 18–21.

Ask: This chapter is called "Harry's First Try." What do you think Harry is trying to do? Answers will vary.

Open and fold back the page to see **3**.

3

Point to the word *down* on page 18.

Ask: Do you think the *ow* in this word says /ow/ or /ō/?

Explain that students can figure out which sound is correct by reading the word both ways, /down/ and /dōn/, and listening for which sounds right.

Explain that Harry thinks the cows' mooing sounds like beautiful music.

Track with your finger and read aloud the first sentence on page 21.

Ask: Do you remember how the lady next door sings? loud and high How does the cows' mooing sound? soft and low Which do you think Harry likes better? the cows' mooing soft and low

Preview pages 22–25.

Ask: Where do you think Harry is taking the cows? Answers will vary.

Say: Harry has to take the cows through town to get to his house. Let's see what places they pass by on their way.

Read aloud page 23 with students.

Preview pages 26 and 27.

Ask: Who do you think this man is? Possible answers: a farmer; the man who owns the cows

Open and fold back the page to see **4**.

4

Does the man who owns the cows look happy? No Who do you think made him angry? Harry

Point to the word *owned* on page 26.

Ask: This word has *ow*. How should we read it? Do we say /ownd/ or /ōnd/? /ōnd/

Tell students that they will now read aloud the chapters to you, but you are there if they need help.

Note: If students have trouble reading on their own, offer one of the following levels of support to meet their needs.

- Read aloud the chapters to them.
- Read aloud the chapters as they chime in with you.
- Take turns with students and alternate reading aloud each page.

Remind students to track with their finger as they read.

Tell students that as they read they should look for the ways that Harry tries to solve his problem and what happens to Harry after each time he tries to solve his problem.

Explore *Harry and the Lady Next Door* (A)

Harry's Problem and Solution Chart

Fill out a row in the chart after you read each chapter in *Harry and the Lady Next Door*.

Harry's Problem: _____

LITERATURE & COMPREHENSION

	How does Harry try to solve the problem?	Does it work?	What happens to Harry?
"Harry's First Try"			
"Harry's Second Try"			
"The Contest"			

Explore *Harry and the Lady Next Door* (B)
"Harry's Second Try"

Fold the page into thirds so that the section labeled ① is showing. Use an accordion, or Z, fold (see the diagram). Use this Reading Aid to preview "Harry's Second Try" in *Harry and the Lady Next Door* with students.

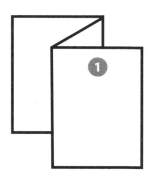

---

①

Preview "Harry's Second Try" with students. Stop at the points indicated and follow the instructions. Answers to questions may vary.

Preview pages 28 and 29.

Ask: Why do you think this chapter is called "Harry's Second Try"?

Why do you think Harry and the cat look unhappy on page 28? The lady next door is singing again.

Explain that Harry goes for a walk to get away from the lady's singing and hears a wonderful sound.

Ask: What do you think could be making that sound?

Point to and read aloud the words *Oompah! Oompah!* on page 29.

Preview pages 30 and 31.

Point to the tuba in the picture and explain that this instrument is called "the big horn" in the story, and that is what's making the wonderful sound.

Ask: Do you think that Harry likes the sound? Yes   How can you tell? He's smiling.

Flip over to see **②**.

3

Tell students that they will now read aloud the chapter to you, but you are there if they need help.

Note: If students have trouble reading on their own, offer one of the following levels of support to meet their needs.

- Read aloud the chapter to them.
- Read aloud the chapter as they chime in with you.
- Take turns with students and alternate reading aloud each page.

Remind students to track with their finger as they read.

Remind students that as they read they should look for how Harry continues to try solving his problem.

2

Preview pages 32–35.

Ask: What does Harry have in his mouth? The bandleader's stick.

Why do you think the band is running after Harry?

Explain that the band is the Firemen's Band and Harry is going to lead the band through town, just like he did with the cows. They will pass by the same places.

Have students track with their finger and read aloud the last sentence on page 35.

Ask: Where do you think Harry is taking the band?

Preview pages 36–39.

Point to the picture on pages 36 and 37 and ask: Where does Harry take the band? to the lady's house

Why do you think Harry wants to bring the band to the lady's house?

Point to the picture on page 38, and ask: Do you think the bandleader is happy with Harry? No

Open and fold back the page to see **3**.

Explore *Harry and the Lady Next Door* (C)
"The Contest"

Fold the page into thirds so that the section labeled
1 is showing. Use an accordion, or Z, fold (see the
diagram). Use this Reading Aid to preview "The Contest"
in *Harry and the Lady Next Door* with students.

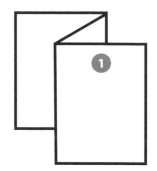

LITERATURE &
COMPREHENSION

1

Preview "The Contest" with students.
Stop at the points indicated and follow the
instructions. Answers to questions may vary.

....

Preview pages 40 and 41.

Explain that at the beginning of this chapter,
Harry's family takes him to the park to hear
the Firemen's Band.

Ask: Do you think Harry likes the Firemen's
Band? Yes   How can you tell? He's smiling.

Point to the word *nights* at the top of
page 41 and explain that the spelling
pattern *igh* makes the long *i* sound.

Ask: If the letters *igh* say /ī/, what is this
word? *nights*

Explain that this is the same spelling pattern
that they've seen in the word *high* every time
the story has said that the lady sings "high
and loud."

Preview pages 42 and 43.

Point to the picture on page 42 and explain
that the man is announcing that the band is
not going to play and, instead, there will be a
singing contest.

Ask: Why do you think Harry is running
away? He sees the lady next door.

Flip over to see **2**.

3

Point to the picture on pages 58 and 59 and explain that the lady next door is going away on a big ship.

Ask: Why do you think she's going away? Where might she be going?

Tell students that they will now read aloud the chapter to you, but you are there if they need help.

Note: If students have trouble reading on their own, offer one of the following levels of support to meet their needs.

- Read aloud the chapter to them.
- Read aloud the chapter as they chime in with you.
- Take turns with students and alternate reading aloud each page.

Remind students to track with their finger as they read.

Tell students that as they read they should look for the reason that the lady next door is on the big ship. They should also think about how Harry finally solves his problem.

2

Preview pages 44–47.

Explain that Harry hears another sound that he thinks is low and beautiful.

Point to and read aloud the words *Blurp Blurp* on page 44.

Ask: What do you think could be making that sound?

Point to the picture on page 46 and explain that the thing Harry is looking into is a watering can.

Can you find the words *watering can* on page 46?

Where do you think Harry is taking the watering can?

Preview pages 48–51.

Ask: Why do you think the ladies are running away? because of the frogs

Do you think the lady next door will run away, too?

Preview pages 52–62.

Point to the picture on pages 54 and 55 and ask: Why do you think everyone is clapping?

Open and fold back the page to see **3**.

Explore Poems About Creative Characters

"I Liked Growing" and "I Had a Dream Last Night"

Fold the page into thirds so that the section labeled **1** is showing. Use an accordion, or Z, fold (see the diagram). Use this Reading Aid to preview "I Liked Growing" and "I Had a Dream Last Night" with students.

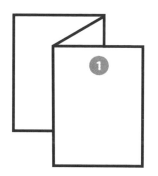

1

Preview "I Liked Growing" and "I Had a Dream Last Night" with students. Stop at the points indicated and follow the instructions. Answers to questions may vary.

·······························

Preview "I Liked Growing."

Ask: The poem is called "I Liked Growing." Who or what do you think is saying that it liked growing in the poem?

Point to the picture on page 96.

Ask: What kind of fruit is this? a strawberry

Can you find the word *strawberry* toward the end of the poem?

Point to the word *leaves* in line 3.

Ask: If the *ea* says /ē/, what is this word? *leaves*

Explain that the *ea* spelling pattern in this word makes the long *e* sound.

Point to the word *cream* toward the end of the poem.

Ask: This word also has the *ea* spelling pattern. What is this word? *cream*

Flip over to see **2**.

3

Tell students that they will now read aloud the poems to you, but you are there if they need help.

Note: If students have trouble reading on their own, offer one of the following levels of support to meet their needs.

- Read aloud the poems to them.
- Read aloud the poems as they chime in with you.
- Take turns with students and alternate reading aloud each line.

Remind students to track with their finger as they read.

Tell students that in each of the poems, the narrator is a character in the poem. As they read each poem, they should think about who is narrating it.

2

Preview "I Had a Dream Last Night."

Ask: Whom do you think this poem is about? Who had a dream?

Point to the word *dream* in line 1.

Explain that this word also has the *ea* spelling pattern that makes the long *e* sound.

Ask: What is this word? *dream*

Explain to students that the character in the poem dreams that she has to choose parents.

Ask: Can you find the word *parents* on page 103?

Open and fold back the page to see **3** .

Explore Poems About Creative Characters
Imagine You Are Something Else

Fill in the blanks to describe what you are.

I Am _____

by _____

I live _____.

I have _____.

I like _____.

I am glad that I am _____!

Explore "Over in the Meadow"

"Over in the Meadow"

Fold the page into thirds so that the section labeled ① is showing. Use an accordion, or Z, fold (see the diagram). Use this Reading Aid to preview "Over in the Meadow" with students.

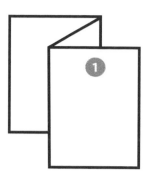

①

Preview "Over in the Meadow" with students. Stop at the points indicated and follow the instructions. Answers to questions may vary.

. . . .

Preview page 216.

Explain that this poem is called "Over in the Meadow" and the first line of each stanza will repeat the title.

STOP **Have students read aloud** the first line of the poem.

Point to the picture on page 216.

Say: This animal that looks like a frog is called a toad.

Ask: Can you find the word *toad* in the first stanza?

Point to the fifth line and ask: What does the mother toad tell the little toad to do? wink

What punctuation mark do you see after the word *wink*? an exclamation mark How should you say the word *wink* when you read the poem? in a strong voice; with a lot of expression

Explain that students should watch for exclamation marks and use a lot of expression when the mother animals speak.

Flip over to see ②*.*

4

Tell students that they will now read aloud the poem to you, but you will help them if they need it.

Note: If students have trouble reading on their own, offer one of the following levels of support to meet their needs.

- Read aloud the poem to them.
- Read aloud the poem as they chime in with you.
- Take turns with students and alternate reading aloud each line or stanza.

Remind students to track with their finger as they read.

Encourage students to stress the words on which the beat falls, so that they read the poem with the appropriate rhythm.

3

Preview page 219.

Explain that there are several words in this stanza with the short *u* sound. Short *u* says /ŭ/.

Point to the word *snug* in line 2.

Ask: The *u* in this word makes the /ŭ/ sound, so what is the word? *snug*

Do you see any other words in this stanza that have the letter *u*? Students should point out the words *buzz, buzzed, hummed.*

How should we read these words?: *buzz, buzzed, hummed*

Tell students that, like many of the other poems they've listened to and read before, this poem has a certain rhythm, or beat.

STOP **Turn back to page 216 and model** how to read lines 1–4 of the first stanza with the appropriate rhythm. Stress the syllables and words that are highlighted. Clap on the beat to help students hear the rhythm. Read the lines again and have students clap with you.

O – ver in the mea – dow,

In the sand, in the sun,

Lived an old mother toad

And her little toadie one.

Open and fold back the page to see **4**.

2

Preview page 217.

Ask: The second stanza is about fish that live in a stream. Can you find the word *stream*?

Explain that the *ea* spelling pattern in *stream* makes the long *e* sound.

Point to the word *leaped* at the end of line 7.

Ask: If the *ea* in this word also makes the /ē/ sound, what is the word? *leaped*

Preview page 218.

Remind students that sometimes they will come across a longer word. One strategy for figuring out that word is to look for a smaller word that they recognize within the longer word.

Point to the word *bluebird* in the third stanza and help students decode the word.

Ask: Do you see any words within this longer word that you recognize?

If students have trouble picking out the words *blue* and *bird*, help them by covering up the word *bird* with your finger so that only the word *blue* is visible. Then cover the word *blue* so that only the word *bird* is visible.

Open and fold back the page to see **3**.

LANGUAGE ARTS GREEN

Explore "Over in the Meadow"
Add the Next Stanza to the Poem

Fill in the blanks to complete the stanza.

Over in the meadow,

In a _____ made of sticks

Lived a mother _____

And her little _____ _____ .

"_____ !" said the mother;

"We _____ ," said the _____ .

So, they _____ and they _____

In the _____ made of sticks.

LITERATURE & COMPREHENSION

Explore *Little Bear* (A)
"What Will Little Bear Wear?"

Fold the page into thirds so that the section labeled ➊ is showing. Use an accordion, or Z, fold (see the diagram). Use this Reading Aid to preview "What Will Little Bear Wear?" in *Little Bear* with students.

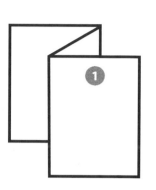

➊

Preview "What Will Little Bear Wear?" with students. Stop at the points indicated and follow the instructions. Answers to questions may vary.

Preview pages 11–13.

STOP **Have students read aloud the** title of the story.

Ask: Look at the picture on page 11. What's the weather like? It's snowing.

Explain that Little Bear is going to say to his mother, "I am cold."

Ask: What do you think that Little Bear might want to wear if it's snowing and he feels cold?

Point to the picture on page 13 and ask: What is on Little Bear's head? a hat

Can you find the word *hat* on page 13?

Point to and read aloud the word *Hurray* on page 13. Explain that the spelling pattern *ay* makes the long *a* sound, like in the words *day* and *play*.

Ask: What punctuation mark do you see after the word *hurray*? an exclamation mark How should you say the word *hurray* when you read it? in a strong voice; with a lot of expression

Flip over to see ➋.

③

Preview pages 18 and 19.

Point to the picture on page 18 and ask: Little Bear still looks cold. What else do you think he could put on?

Explain that Little Bear's mother is going to offer Little Bear a fur coat to keep warm.

Track with your finger and read aloud the last sentence on page 19.

Ask: Do you think that a fur coat will help Little Bear keep warm?

Tell students that they will now read aloud the story to you, but you will help them if they need it.

Note: If students have trouble reading on their own, offer one of the following levels of support to meet their needs.

- Read aloud the story to them.
- Read aloud the story as they chime in with you.
- Take turns with students and alternate reading aloud each page.

Remind students to track with their finger as they read.

Encourage students to think about the elements that make up a story as they read—characters, setting, and problem and solution—so they can retell the story after they read.

---

②

Preview pages 14 and 15.

Remind students that if they come across a word they don't know, they can look at the first letter of the word and then look at the picture to see if there's something in the picture that starts with that letter.

Practice the strategy with students. Point to the word *coat* on page 15.

Ask: What letter is at the beginning of this word? *c*   Do you see something in the picture on page 15 that starts with the letter *c*? a coat

Note: If students don't notice the coat, prompt them by asking, "What new piece of clothing is Little Bear wearing?"

Preview pages 16 and 17.

Ask: What else do you think Little Bear will put on here?

Point to the picture on page 17 and ask: What new piece of clothing does Little Bear have on? pants

Can you find the word *pants* on page 17?

Open and fold back the page to see **③** .

Explore *Little Bear* (A)

Retell "What Will Little Bear Wear?"

Cut out the characters and clothes, and then use them to retell the story.

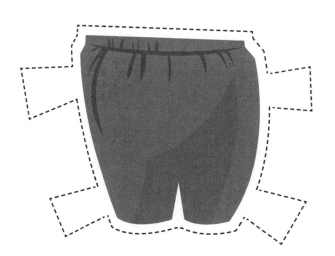

LITERATURE & COMPREHENSION

Explore *Little Bear* (B)

"Birthday Soup" and "Little Bear Goes to the Moon"

Fold the page into thirds so that the section labeled
1 is showing. Use an accordion, or Z, fold (see the
diagram). Use this Reading Aid to preview "Birthday
Soup" and "Little Bear Goes to the Moon" in *Little Bear*
with students.

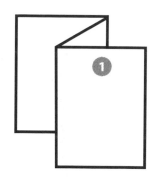

Preview "Birthday Soup" and "Little Bear Goes to the Moon" with students. Stop at the points indicated and follow the instructions. Answers to questions may vary.

· · · · · · · · · · · · · · · · · · ·

Preview pages 22 and 23.

STOP **Have students read aloud the** title of the story.

Ask: Whose birthday do you think it is?

Explain that it is Little Bear's birthday, but he doesn't know where his mother is and he doesn't see a birthday cake. So he decides to make soup for his friends.

Ask: What do you think that Little Bear might put in his soup?

Point to and read aloud the last line on page 23.

Preview pages 24–31.

Explain that Little Bear's friends are arriving to help him celebrate his birthday.

Ask: Who are Little Bear's friends? a hen; a duck; a cat

Flip over to see **2** *.*

1

4

Tell students that they will now read aloud the stories to you, but you will help them if they need it.

Note: If students have trouble reading on their own, offer one of the following levels of support to meet their needs.

- Read aloud the stories to them.
- Read aloud the stories as they chime in with you.
- Take turns with students and alternate reading aloud each page.

Remind students to track with their finger as they read.

Encourage students to think about what happens in the beginning, middle, and end of each story as they read.

3

Preview pages 38–41.

Explain that Little Bear thinks he can fly like a bird. But Mother Bear tells Little Bear that he doesn't have wings or feathers.

Ask: Can you find the word *feathers* on page 38?

Explain that Little Bear believes if he jumps from a high spot, he'll fly up.

Point to the picture on page 41 and ask: What high spot do you think Little Bear will jump from? a tree

Preview pages 42–49.

Ask: After Little Bear comes down, the story says that he *tumbled*. Can you find the word *tumbled* on page 42?

Track with your finger and read aloud the last sentence on page 42.

Ask: Do you think that Little Bear is pretending that he's on the moon, or does he really believe it?

What will Little Bear see while he's on the moon? a house; a table; food; Mother Bear

Point to the picture on page 49 and ask: Do you think Little Bear is happy to see his mother? How can you tell?

Open and fold back the page to see **4**.

2

Preview pages 32–35.

Ask: Do you think that Mother Bear forgot Little Bear's birthday? No   How can you tell? She has a birthday cake.

Do you think that Little Bear is surprised by the birthday cake?

Explain that Mother Bear made the cake as a surprise.

Ask: Can you find the word *surprise* on page 34?

Preview pages 36 and 37.

Ask: What is that on Little Bear's head?

Explain that Little Bear is pretending that he has a space helmet.

Ask: Can you find the words *space helmet* on page 36?

This story is called "Little Bear Goes to the Moon." How do you think Little Bear plans on getting to the moon?

Track with your finger and read aloud the first sentence on page 37.

Ask: Do you think that Little Bear can fly to the moon?

Open and fold back the page to see **3**.

Explore *Little Bear* (C)
Write a Silly Story

Fill in the blanks to complete the story.

_____ is a(n) _____. She is
(girl's name)   (noun–thing)

hungry! But, there are no snacks at home. So, she

_____ to the store to buy _____.
(verb–action word)   (noun–thing)

"This snack is _____!" she said.
                     (adjective–describing word)

"I think I will share it with _____.
                                       (boy's name)

He is a(n) _____. He will eat anything."
               (noun–thing)

And he did!

Explore *Little Bear* (C)
"Little Bear's Wish"

Fold the page into thirds so that the section labeled ❶ is showing. Use an accordion, or Z, fold (see the diagram). Use this Reading Aid to preview "Little Bear's Wish" in *Little Bear* with students.

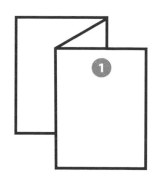

❶

Preview "Little Bear's Wish" with students. Stop at the points indicated and follow the instructions. Answers to questions may vary.

....

Preview pages 50 and 51.

STOP **Have students read aloud** the title of the story.

Ask: What do you think Little Bear might wish for?

Do you think this story is happening during the day or at night? at night How can you tell? Little Bear is in bed; there's a candle in the picture.

Preview pages 52–56.

Explain that Little Bear is going to make wishes on these next pages, but his mother will tell him that those wishes aren't possible.

Point to and read aloud the last two lines on page 52.

Explain that Mother Bear will repeat this after all of Little Bear's impossible wishes.

Point to the picture on page 53.

Ask: What kind of boat do you think this is?

Explain that it is a Viking boat.

Flip over to see ❷.

4

Remind students to track with their finger as they read.

Encourage students to think about the important events in the beginning, middle, and end of the story as they read, so that they will be able to retell the story.

3

Preview pages 57–61.

Explain that after all of his impossible wishes, Little Bear is going to wish to hear a story.

Ask: Do you think that Little Bear can have that wish?   What kind of story do you think Little Bear will want to hear?
Yes

Point to the pictures on pages 58 and 59 and ask: Do these pictures look familiar? Where have you seen them before? in the other *Little Bear* stories

Based on these pictures, what kind of stories do you think Mother Bear will tell? Who will the stories be about? Little Bear

Tell students that they will now read aloud the story to you, but you will help them if they need it.

Note: If students have trouble reading on their own, offer one of the following levels of support to meet their needs.

- Read aloud the story to them.
- Read aloud the story as they chime in with you.
- Take turns with students and alternate reading aloud each page.

Open and fold back the page to see **4**.

2

Ask: Can you find the word *Viking* on page 53?

Explain that after Little Bear wishes for a Viking boat, he wishes to go all the way to China through a tunnel.

Point to and read aloud the word *China* on page 54.

Explain that China is a very large country and the word *China* begins with a capital letter because it is the name of a country.

Point to the picture on page 55 and ask: What kind of building is this? a castle

Can you find the word *castle* on page 55?

Why do you think we'll see the word *castle* in this story? because it's part of Little Bear's wishes

Point to the picture on page 56 and ask: Who do you think this person might be? a princess

Can you find the word *princess* on page 56?

Open and fold back the page to see **3**.

LANGUAGE ARTS GREEN

Explore *Little Bear* (C)
Definition Map: Fiction

Answer the questions in the boxes about fiction text.

What is it?	What is it like?

Fiction

What are some examples?

Introduce "Little Bears"
Tell Fact from Fiction

Read the two paragraphs. Then, tell which one is fact, or nonfiction.

Paragraph 1

Gus is a dog. He likes to sniff things. One day, Gus sniffed a flower. Gus started to bark, and then he ran away. Why did Gus run away? There was a big bee in the flower that yelled, "Hey! Get that big nose out of my face!"

Paragraph 2

A dog has a strong nose. A dog can use its nose to smell things that a person cannot smell. Did you know that a dog's nose also helps a dog keep cool? That is because a dog sweats through its nose!

Introduce "Little Bears"

"Little Bears"

Fold the page into thirds so that the section labeled ❶ is showing. Use an accordion, or Z, fold (see the diagram). Use this Reading Aid to preview "Little Bears" with students.

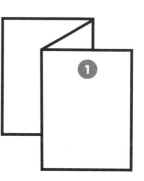

Preview "Little Bears" with students. Stop at the points indicated and follow the instructions. Answers to questions may vary.

Preview pages 16 and 17.

STOP **Have students read aloud** the title of the article.

Explain that this article is nonfiction.

Ask: What things do you see on these pages that tell you this article is nonfiction? *pictures of real bears; a caption*

How do you think it will be different from the *Little Bear* stories: Will it be a made-up story or about real things? *about real things*

Remind students that if they come across a word they don't know, they can look for a smaller word or word part that they know inside the word.

Point to the word *insects* in the first paragraph.

Ask: Do you see any words or word parts within this word that you recognize?

If students have trouble picking out the word *in*, help them by covering up the rest of the word so that only the word *in* shows.

Explain that once students have figured out part of the word, they can try sounding out the rest of the word.

❶

LANGUAGE ARTS GREEN   **LC 321**

2

Ask: What is this word? *insects*

Preview pages 18–21.

Ask: What are some things that you see on these pages that tell us this is a nonfiction article? Possible answers: a heading; pictures; captions; words in bold print

Point to the heading on page 18 and **ask:** What time of year do you think this section will be about? winter

Point to the word *cubs* in bold print on page 19.

Ask: Why do you think this word is in bold print? It's an important word.

Why do you think the word *cubs* is an important word in this article? What is the article about? It's about baby bears; it's about bear cubs.

Point to the word *out* in the first paragraph on page 19, and remind students that the *ou* in *out* says /ow/.

Point to the word *ground* in the first paragraph on page 19.

Ask: If the *ou* says /ow/, what do you think this word is? *ground*

Open and fold back the page to see **3** *.*

3

Explain that students should watch for other words in the article with the *ou* that says /ow/.

Preview pages 22–25.

Point to the heading on page 23 and ask: What time of year do you think this section will be about? spring

What do you notice about the cubs in these pictures? How have they changed? They're bigger; they've grown.

Point to the picture on page 24 and ask: What are the cubs doing? climbing a tree

Can you find the word *climb* in the first paragraph of page 24?

Preview pages 26 and 27.

Point to the heading on page 27 and ask: What time of year do you think this section will be about? summer

Point to the word *eat* in the first paragraph on page 26, and remind students that the *ea* in *eat* says /ē/.

Point to and read aloud the word *teaches* in the first paragraph on page 26, and explain that this is another example of a word in which *ea* makes the long *e* sound. Explain that students should watch for even more words with the *ea* that says /ē/.

Open and fold back the page to see **4** *.*

4

Preview pages 28 and 29.

Point to the heading on page 29 and ask: What time of year do you think this section will be about? spring

Explain that part of the heading says, "One year later."

Ask: How do you think the bear cubs will have changed in that year?

Tell students that they will now read aloud the article to you, but you will help them if they need it.

Note: If students have trouble reading on their own, offer one of the following levels of support to meet their needs.

- Read aloud the article to them.
- Read aloud the article as they chime in with you.
- Take turns with students and alternate reading aloud each paragraph or page.

Remind students to track with their finger as they read.

Tell students that as they read, they should think about the features of the article that let them know it is nonfiction and about real things.

Introduce "Little Bears"

Bears: Fact and Fiction

Compare the bear cubs in the article "Little Bears" to the cub in the book *Little Bear*.

Little Bear

Both

"Little Bears"

LITERATURE & COMPREHENSION

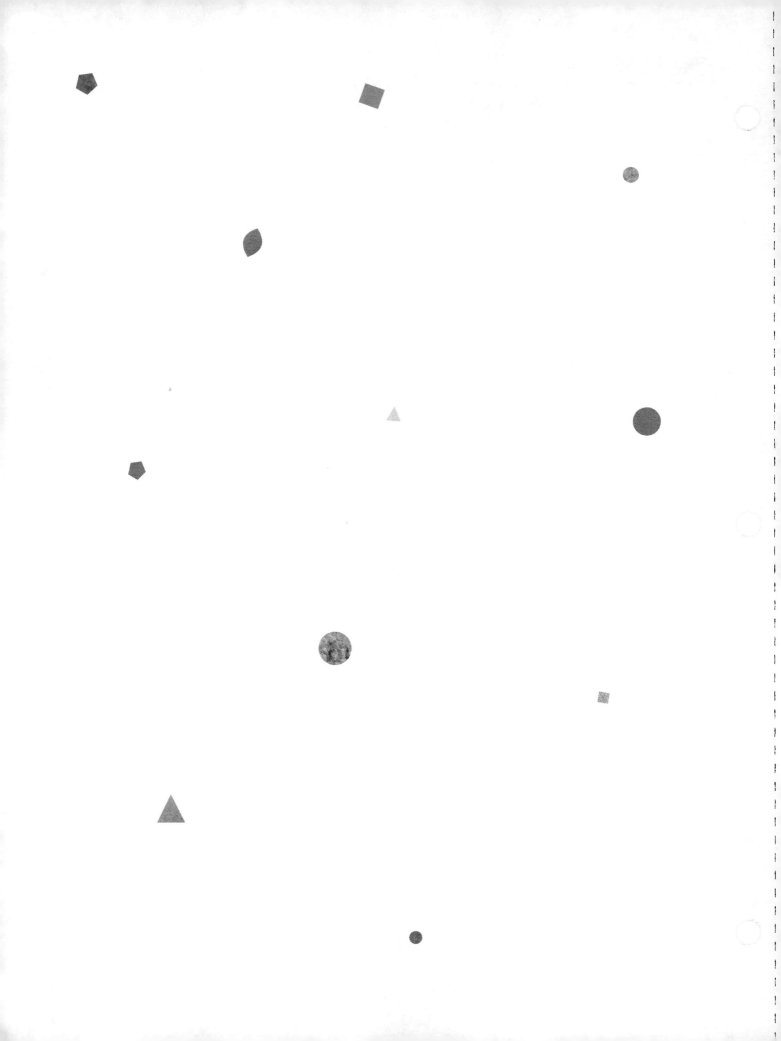

Explore *Owl at Home* (A)
"The Guest" and "Strange Bumps"

Fold the page into thirds so that the section labeled ❶ is showing. Use an accordion, or Z, fold (see the diagram). Use this Reading Aid to preview "The Guest" and "Strange Bumps" in *Owl at Home* with students.

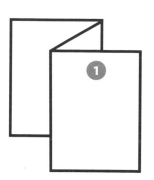

Flip over to see ❷.

Point to the word *eating* near the bottom of page 5 and have students practice the strategy. Have them cover the *–ing* with their finger and read the base word *eat*. Then have them uncover the *–ing* and read the whole word.

Explain that in this story students will see many verbs, or action words, with the word part *–ing* at the end. If students are not sure how to read the word, they can try the strategy of covering up the *–ing,* so they can see just the base word without the ending.

Ask: Can you find the word *sitting* on page 5?

Explain that Owl is sitting by the fire, eating his supper.

Ask: Who do you think the guest might be?

Look at the pictures. What's the weather like? It's snowing; it's cold.   Is it day or night? night

STOP **Have students read aloud** the title of the story.

Preview pages 4–7.

Preview "The Guest" and "Strange Bumps" with students. Stop at the points indicated and follow the instructions. Answers to questions may vary.

❶

LITERATURE & COMPREHENSION

❹

Preview pages 26–29.

Ask: What is happening in the pictures on these pages?

Do you think that Owl will ever figure out what is making those bumps?

Tell students that they will now read aloud the stories to you, but you will help them if they need it.

Note: If students have trouble reading on their own, offer one of the following levels of support to meet their needs.

- Read aloud the stories to them.

- Read aloud the stories as they chime in with you.

- Take turns with students and alternate reading aloud each page.

Remind students to track with their finger as they read.

Encourage students to think about the elements that make up a story as they read—characters, setting, and problem and solution—so that they can retell the stories after they read.

---

❸

Track with your finger and read aloud the last sentence on page 19.

Preview pages 20 and 21.

Explain that students will see some verbs, or action words, with the word part –ed at the end. If students are not sure how to read the word, they can try covering up the –ed, so that they can see just the base word.

Point to the word lifted at the top of page 20 and have students practice the strategy. Have them cover the –ed with their finger and read the base word lift. Then have them uncover the –ed and read the whole word.

Preview pages 22–25.

Ask: Do you think that Owl will figure out what is causing the strange bumps?

Tell students that Owl is getting more and more worried about those bumps. When we read the sentences that Owl says, we should hear that worry in his voice.

Point to and read aloud the sentence "One of those bumps is moving!" in an exaggerated, worried voice.

Ask: When Owl says this, what punctuation mark do you see?   exclamation mark   How do we read sentences that end with exclamation marks? in a loud voice; with emphasis

Tell students that as they read, they should look for exclamation marks and think about how Owl would sound as he's speaking.

Open and fold back the page to see **❹** *.*

---

❷

Preview pages 6–9.

Tell students that many words in this story have the / ow / sound, which can be spelled two ways. It can be spelled ow as in how and ou as in out. The first sentence on page 6 has words with both these spelling patterns.

STOP **Have students read aloud** the first sentence on page 6. Help students locate the words with the ow and the ou spelling patterns.

Ask: In which season do you think this story is happening? winter   Can you find the word winter on page 8?

Preview pages 10–17.

Ask: What is happening in these pictures? What do you think is Owl's problem?

There is a lot of snow in Owl's house. Can you find the word snow at the top of page 13?

Preview pages 18 and 19.

Read aloud the story title.

Point to the picture on page 18 and ask: What do you think is making the strange bumps? How do you think Owl is feeling about the bumps?

Explain that Owl doesn't know what is causing the bumps.

Open and fold back the page to see **❸** *.*

Explore *Owl at Home* (B)

"Tear-Water Tea" and "Upstairs and Downstairs"

Fold the page into thirds so that the section labeled ❶ is showing. Use an accordion, or Z, fold (see the diagram). Use this Reading Aid to preview "Tear-Water Tea" and "Upstairs and Downstairs" in *Owl at Home* with students.

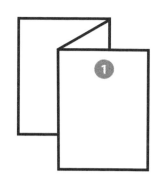

Preview "Tear-Water Tea" and "Upstairs and Downstairs" with students. Stop at the points indicated and follow the instructions. Answers to questions may vary.

Preview pages 30 and 31.

Read aloud the title of the story.

Ask: How do you think somebody would make tear-water tea?

Explain that Owl is holding a kettle to make his tea.

Ask: Can you find the word *kettle* at the top of page 31?

Owl is thinking about things that make him feel sad. What are some things that make you feel sad?

Preview pages 32–35.

Explain that the pictures on these pages will give a lot of information about what's happening in the story and what words students will see.

Ask: What do you see in the picture on page 32? Possible answers: chairs; broken chairs

Have students read aloud the first sentence on page 32.

Ask: Looking at the pictures on these pages, what are some words you might read in the story that are related to the pictures?

❶

Flip over to see ❷.

2

Preview pages 36–39.

Ask: What is Owl using to fill up his kettle to make tea? *tears* Can you find the word *tears* on page 37?

What do you think tea made with tears would taste like?

How do you think Owl is feeling as he drinks his tea?

Preview pages 40 and 41.

Read aloud the story title.

Explain that this story will have many compound words in it. A compound word is a word that is made up of two smaller words.

Point to and read aloud the word *upstairs* in the title.

Ask: What two words make up the compound word *upstairs*? *up* and *stairs*

Tell students that if they are not sure how to read a longer word, they can check to see if the word has a shorter word they recognize that is part of the longer word.

Point to the word *bedroom* near the bottom of page 41 and have students practice the strategy.

Open and fold back the page to see **3**.

3

Ask: Do you see any words that you recognize in this longer word?

Note: If students have trouble seeing the words *bed* and *room*, cover up *room* so they can see just the word *bed*, and then cover the word *bed* so they can see just *room*.

Preview pages 42–47.

Ask: What do you think Owl is doing in this part of the story?

Why do you think he's doing that?

Preview pages 48 and 49.

Explain that Owl is sitting in the middle of his stairs.

Ask: Why do you think he's doing that?

Can you find the word *middle* at the bottom of page 49?

Tell students that they will now read aloud the stories to you, but you will help them if they need it.

Open and fold back the page to see **4**.

4

Note: If students have trouble reading on their own, offer one of the following levels of support to meet their needs.

- Read aloud the stories to them.
- Read aloud the stories as they chime in with you.
- Take turns with students and alternate reading aloud each page.

Remind students to track with their finger as they read.

Encourage students to think about the following questions as they read.

- Do the stories remind them of anything? What connections can they make?
- Does Owl have a problem in either story and what does he do to try and solve it?

Explore *Owl at Home* (C)
"Owl and the Moon"

Fold the page into thirds so that the section labeled ❶ is showing. Use an accordion, or Z, fold (see the diagram). Use this Reading Aid to preview "Owl and the Moon" in *Owl at Home* with students.

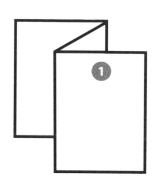

❶

Preview "Owl and the Moon" with students. Stop at the points indicated and follow the instructions. Answers to questions may vary.

Preview pages 50 and 51.

Have students read aloud the title of the story.

Ask: Do you think this story is happening during the day or at night? at night

Can you find the word *night* at the top of page 51?

Preview pages 52 and 53.

Ask: Who do you think Owl is talking to?

Explain that this story has many words with the long *i* sound.

Point to and read aloud the word *climbed* in line 2 of page 52.

Explain that *climbed* is one word with the /ī/ sound. It is a tough word because the letter *b* is silent.

Point to the word *higher* in line 2 of page 52.

Remind students that the *igh* spelling pattern makes the long *i* sound.

Ask: If *igh* says /ī/, what is this word? *higher*

Flip over to see ❷.

2

Point to the word *whole* in line 4 of page 52.

Explain that this is another difficult word because the letter *w* is silent.

Ask: If the *w* at the beginning of this word is silent, what is the word? *whole*

Preview pages 54–59.

Point to the word *sky* near the bottom of page 54.

Tell students that this is another word with the long *i* sound. In this word, the letter *y* makes the long *i* sound.

Ask: What is this word? *sky*

Explain that in this part of the story Owl thinks the moon is following him.

Ask: Can you find the word *following* at the bottom of page 54?

What do you think Owl is saying to the moon in this part of the story?

Open and fold back the page to see **3** *.*

3

Preview pages 60 and 61.

Explain that sometimes when we have trouble reading a word, we can try the following steps:

1. Skip the unknown word and read to the end of the sentence.
2. Look for any word parts in the unknown word that we recognize.
3. Think about what word would make sense.
4. Reread the sentence from the beginning and see if the word we decided on makes sense.

Point to the first sentence on page 60 and tell students that you will model this strategy.

Read aloud: "The moon went [blank] some clouds."

Say: I recognize the word part *be* in this word. I think that the word *behind* would make sense because I know that the moon can go behind clouds.

Reread the sentence aloud: "The moon went behind some clouds."

Ask: Does the word *behind* make sense?

Open and fold back the page to see **4** *.*

4

Preview pages 62–64.

Point to the word *round* near the bottom of page 62.

Remind students that the *ou* spelling pattern makes the / ow / sound.

Ask: What is this word? *round*

Tell students that they will now read aloud the story to you, but you will help them if they need it.

Note: If students have trouble reading on their own, offer one of the following levels of support to meet their needs.

*   Read aloud the story to them.
*   Read aloud the story as they chime in with you.
*   Take turns with students and alternate reading aloud each page.

Remind students to track with their finger as they read.

Encourage students to think about the following as they read:

*   How does Owl make the moon sound like it's a person?
*   What are the elements in the story— the characters, setting, and problem and solution?

Explore *Owl at Home* (C)
Retell "Owl and the Moon"

Use the Retelling Hand to help retell a story.

Explore *Owl at Home* (C)

Create a Features of Fiction Poster

Follow the instructions to make a Features of Fiction poster.

1. Write "Features of Fiction" at the top of the poster board.

2. Print the story elements on index cards.

3. Print the names of text features you might find in a fiction story on the cards.

4. Glue the cards to the poster board.

5. Cut out pictures to go with the story elements and text features.

6. Draw or glue cutout pictures that stand for story elements and features. Draw or glue them near the card for that element or feature.

Introduce "Hunters of the Night"
"Hunters of the Night"

Fold the page into thirds so that the section labeled ❶ is showing. Use an accordion, or Z, fold (see the diagram). Use this Reading Aid to preview "Hunters of the Night" with students.

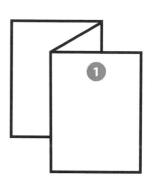

❶

Preview "Hunters of the Night" with students. Stop at the points indicated and follow the instructions. Answers to questions may vary.

Preview pages 30 and 31.

STOP **Have students read aloud** the title of the article.

Ask: What things do you see on these pages that tell you this article is a nonfiction article about real things? pictures of real owls; captions

What are some words that you could use to describe a real owl?

Point to and read aloud the first sentence on page 31.

Explain that this sentences describes an owl as "shadowy" and says that an owl "flies silently."

Ask: What other types of information do you think the article will tell us about owls?

Say: I see the phrase *burrowing owls*, but I'm not sure what a burrowing owl is. I can try to figure it out from the information around it.

Read aloud the last two sentences on page 30.

Flip over to see **❷**.

2

Say: The word *dug* is a clue. Because burrowing owls live in burrows dug by other animals, I think that burrowing owls are owls that live in holes in the ground. Using the words and sentences around an unknown word is one strategy we can use to figure out what a word or phrase means.

Preview pages 32–35.

Explain that the picture on page 32 has circles around certain parts of the owl's body so that readers will notice them. The things that are special about an owl are called features.

Ask: Can you find the word *features* in the second paragraph on page 32?

Point to the pictures and title of the sidebar, "Big and Small."

Ask: What do you think this section of the article might be about?

Why do you think these owls are shown next to a bat and a hand?

Point to the picture of the owl's eyes on page 34.

Ask: What feature of owls do you think this part of the article might talk about? their eyes

Can you find the word *eyes* in the second paragraph on page 34?

Open and fold back the page to see **3**.

3

Say: Let's practice figuring out the meaning of unknown words.

Read aloud the first paragraph on page 35.

Ask: Are there any words in that paragraph that you don't know the meaning of? Students may ask about the words *spot* and *scurrying*.

Help students use context clues to figure out that *spot* means "see" and *scurrying* means "running."

Preview pages 36–39.

Ask: One special feature of owls is their ears. What do you think an owl's ears look like?

Point to and read aloud the second sentence on page 37. "Owls' ears are long, thin openings on either side of their head."

Explain that another special feature of owls is their long, soft feathers.

Ask: Can you find the word *feathers* in the second paragraph of page 37?

Tell students that an owl can fly very quietly because its feathers have soft edges.

Ask: Can you find the word *edges* in the second paragraph on page 38:

Open and fold back the page to see **4**.

4

Preview pages 40 and 41.

Ask: What do you think this section of the article might be about?

What are some words you might expect to see in a section about baby owls?

Note: You may want to point out the following words on page 40, if students do not mention them on their own: *nests, eggs, hatch, mother,* and *father.*

Tell students that they will now read aloud the article to you, but you will help them if they need it.

Note: If students have trouble reading on their own, offer one of the following levels of support to meet their needs.

- Read aloud the article to them.
- Read aloud the article as they chime in with you.
- Take turns with students and alternate reading aloud each paragraph or page.

Remind students to track with their finger as they read.

Tell students that as they read, they should think about things in the article that let them know it is nonfiction. They should also ask questions about any words they don't know the meaning of and use clues around those words to try to figure out the meaning.

Introduce "Hunters of the Night"
Definition Map: Nonfiction

Answer the questions in the boxes about nonfiction text.

What is it?

What is it like?

Nonfiction

What are some examples?

Explore "Hunters of the Night"
Create a Features of Nonfiction Poster

Follow the instructions to make a Features of Nonfiction poster.

1. Write "Features of Nonfiction" at the top of the poster board.

2. Print the names of features you might find in a nonfiction magazine and article on index cards.

3. Glue the cards to the poster board.

4. Cut out examples of the features from old magazines, and glue them near the card for that feature.

Introduce "The Hummingbird and the Butterfly"

"The Hummingbird and the Butterfly"

Fold the page into thirds so that the section labeled **1** is showing. Use an accordion, or Z, fold (see the diagram). Use this Reading Aid to preview "The Hummingbird and the Butterfly" with students.

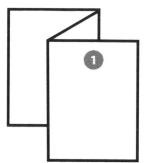

Preview "The Hummingbird and the Butterfly" with students. Stop at the points indicated and follow the instructions. Answers to questions may vary.

· ·

Preview pages 220 and 221.

STOP **Have students read aloud** the title of the play.

Point to the list of characters under the title and explain that when we read a play, the characters' names are always listed at the beginning of the script.

Ask: Based on the title, the pictures, and the list of characters, who do you think will be the main characters in this play? *a hummingbird; a butterfly*

Point to and read aloud the word *Hummingbird* in bold type at the beginning of the first line of dialogue.

Explain that the characters in a play speak out loud. The name in bold type at the beginning of a block of text tells us which character is speaking. The character says the words that come after the name.

Remind students that in a play, the characters' conversation is called the dialogue.

Flip over to see **2**.

1

2

Ask: When the person playing Hummingbird reads his or her lines, does he or she say, "Hummingbird. Look at that beautiful creature over there!"? No   Why doesn't the person playing Hummingbird say the word *hummingbird* out loud? because the word *hummingbird* is there just to tell us which character is speaking

Tell students that Hummingbird thinks that Butterfly is beautiful.

Ask: Can you find the word *beautiful* at the top of page 220?

Explain that Hummingbird also wants to fly together with Butterfly.

Ask: Can you find the word *together* near the bottom of page 220?

Preview pages 222 and 223.

Ask: Can you point to a part of the script in which Butterfly is speaking? Students may point to any line that has **BUTTERFLY** at the beginning.

Explain that Butterfly will tell Hummingbird that he was once a caterpillar.

Ask: Can you find the word *caterpillar* near the top of page 222?

Open and fold back the page to see **3**.

3

Tell students that they will now read aloud the play to you, but you will help them if they need it.

Note: If students have trouble reading on their own, offer one of the following levels of support to meet their needs.

- Read aloud the play to them.
- Read aloud the play as they chime in with you.
- Take turns with students and alternate reading aloud the lines. Have students read one character's lines while you read the other's lines.

Remind students to track with their finger as they read.

Encourage students to think about the features in the text that tell them it is a play with dialogue.

Explore "The Hummingbird and the Butterfly"

Act Out "The Hummingbird and the Butterfly"

Color the characters, and cut them out. Then, glue them to craft sticks, and use them to act out the play.

LITERATURE & COMPREHENSION

Introduce "The Lion and the Mouse"

"The Lion and the Mouse"

Fold the page into thirds so that the section labeled ❶ is showing. Use an accordion, or Z, fold (see the diagram). Use this Reading Aid to preview "The Lion and the Mouse" with students.

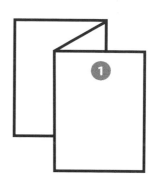

Preview "The Lion and the Mouse" with students. Stop at the points indicated and follow the instructions. Answers to questions may vary.

....

Preview pages 224 and 225.

STOP **Have students read aloud** the title of the play.

Point to the list of characters under the title and remind students that the characters' names are always listed at the beginning of a script.

Ask: Based on the title, the pictures, and the list of characters, who do you think will be the main characters in this play? a lion; a mouse

Point to and read aloud the words *Scene I* below the list of characters.

Explain that plays can be broken up into parts called scenes. This play has two scenes.

Ask: Do you remember the reasons why a play would have different scenes? because the scenes may happen in different places; to show that time has passed between one scene and the next

Point to and read aloud the word *Lion* at the beginning of the first line of dialogue.

Ask: Why is this word here? What does it tell us? Possible answers: The Lion character will be speaking; these are the lines that Lion will say out loud.

❶

2

Point to and read aloud the words *yawning wide* in parentheses after the word *Lion* on page 224.

Ask: Why do you think these words are here? Do you think the actor playing Lion is supposed to say these words out loud?

Explain that these words are called stage directions. They are special instructions that tell actors what they're supposed to do, and the actors do not say these words out loud. Stage directions are usually inside of parentheses and are written in italic, which are slanting letters.

Ask: Why do you think the stage directions tell the Lion character to yawn? to show that he's tired or sleepy   Can you show me what it looks like to yawn wide?

Can you find another example of stage directions on page 225?

Preview pages 226 and 227.

Point to the picture on page 226.

Ask: Who do you think are these two people in the picture?

Explain that the two children are wearing costumes, and they are actors playing the characters of Lion and Mouse.

Open and fold back the page to see **3**.

3

Tell students that the actors are shown on a stage. Plays are usually performed on a stage.

Point to Mouse's lines near the bottom of page 227.

Explain that the stage directions tell us that Mouse is bouncing up and down on Lion's belly. So it's hard for Mouse to speak clearly. We can see that some of the letters in the words are repeated.

Ask: Can you say these lines the way that you think Mouse would sound?

Preview pages 228–233.

Point to and read aloud "Scene II, Two Months Later," at the top of page 228.

Explain that this is the beginning of the second scene. Two months have passed since we last saw Lion and Mouse.

Point to the audience on page 228.

Explain that the people watching the play are called the audience.

Point to Lion's lines on page 228.

Say: I see exclamation marks here. How do you think Lion says these lines? Possible answers: in a loud voice; with a lot of expression.

Open and fold back the page to see **4**.

4

STOP **Have students read aloud** Lion's lines on page 228.

Ask: Why do you think Lion is speaking with a lot of expression? How might he be feeling? He's trapped, so he's probably feeling scared and helpless.

What do you see happening in the rest of the pictures of the play?

Tell students that they will now read aloud the play to you, but you will help them if they need it.

Note: If students have trouble reading on their own, offer one of the following levels of support to meet their needs.

- Read aloud the play to them.
- Read aloud the play as they chime in with you.
- Take turns with students and alternate reading aloud the lines. Have students read one character's lines while you read the other's lines.

Remind students to track with their finger as they read.

Encourage students to think about how the play is different from stories and nonfiction articles that they have read before.

Introduce "The Lion and the Mouse"

Prepare to Act Out a Play

Cut out the masks. Then, glue yarn and string to make a mane and whiskers.

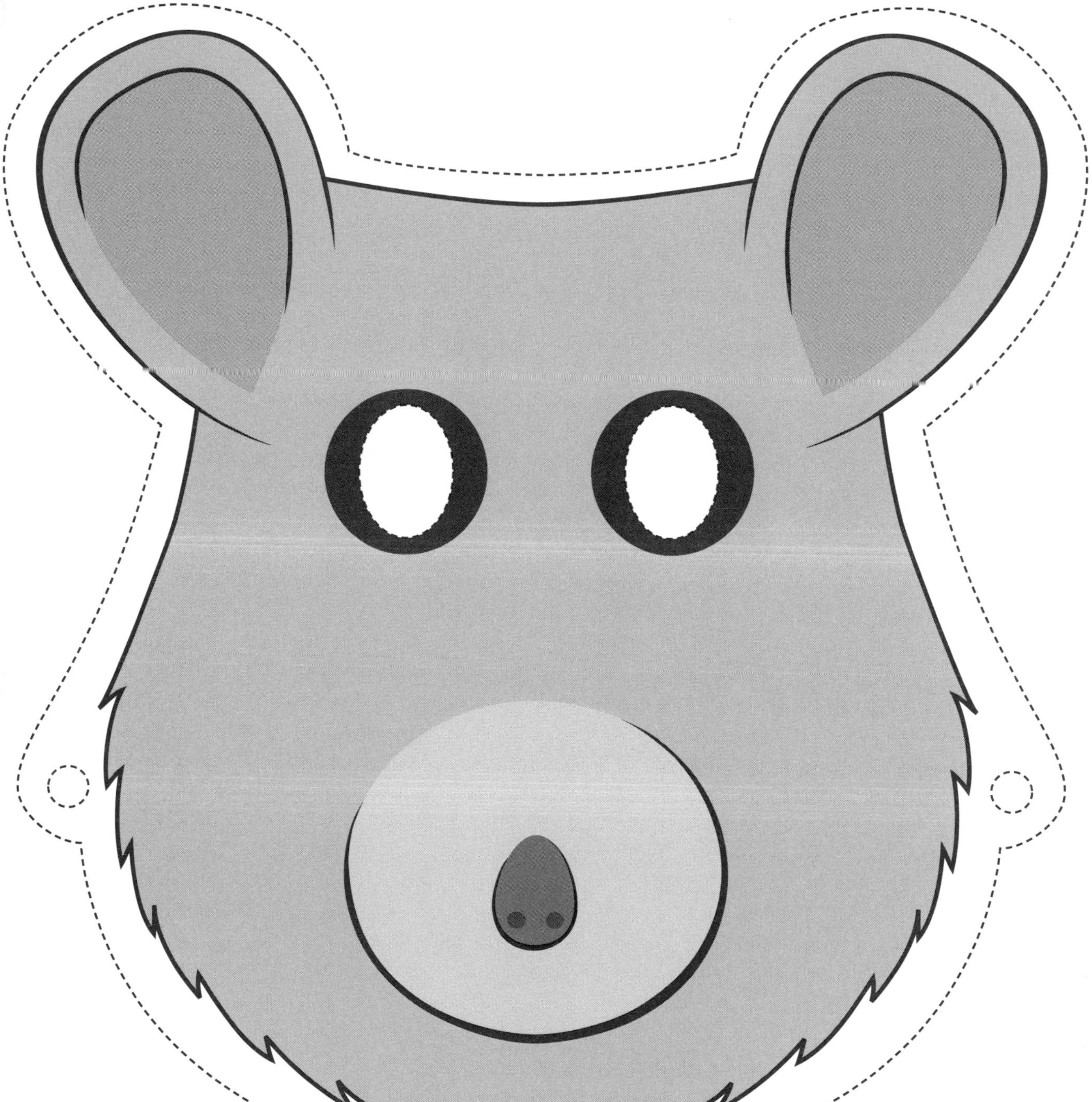

Writing Skills

The Sentence

Sentence Parts

▶ A **sentence** is a complete idea. It has a part that names who or what does something and a part that shows the action.

The monkey **ate a banana.**

↑ naming part   ↑ action part

Draw one line under the naming part and two lines under the action part.

1. Amy skated.

2. My friend Meg skated at the rink.

3. Bill and I played.

4. I fell asleep.

5. Everyone watched the movie.

The Sentence
Make Complete Sentences

Make a check (✓) if the sentence is complete and an X (✗) if the sentence is not complete.

1. Slept on the floor. _____

2. My brother and I heard a loud noise. _____

3. We saw something big. _____

4. Ran from a dinosaur. _____

Write a complete sentence with a naming part and an action part.

5. _____

_____

_____

Sentence Beginnings and Endings
Sentence Hunt

Cut out these word groups.

played in the snow.

I made a snow fort.

The snowman

We drank hot chocolate.

My friend

caught snowflakes with his tongue.

The dog barked.

Sentence Beginnings and Endings
Capital Letters and End Marks

▶ Every sentence begins with a capital letter and ends with an end mark.

The lion wore a hat.

↑ capital letter   ↑ end mark

Who gave the lion that hat?

↑ capital letter   ↑ end mark

Underline the capital letter at the beginning of the sentence, and circle the end mark at the end of the sentence.

1. Marcus plays football.

2. His dog plays basketball.

3. Whose hamster plays hockey?

4. Jimmy's hamster plays hockey.

5. Our pets love sports.

Sentence Beginnings and Endings

Fix Sentences

Do a buddy check to fix each sentence. Write a capital letter at the beginning of the sentence and add an end mark at the end of the sentence. The first one has been done for you.

1. P
   ~~p~~enguins swim in the water.

2. elephants eat peanuts

3. tigers sleep in the sun

4. bears play

5. animals live at the zoo

Write a sentence about the zoo. Be sure to begin with a capital letter and end with an end mark.

6. _____

   _____

   _____

Make the Sentence Bigger
Use Detail Words

Use the words in the word bank to add more detail to the sentence.

WRITING SKILLS

Word Bank				
at	into	on	through	until

1. The elephant sat _____ the stool.

2. My sister laughed _____ the clowns.

3. The man juggled _____ the balls dropped.

4. The lion jumped _____ the hoop.

5. The clowns climbed _____ the car.

Make One from Two
Use Joining Words

Write the correct joining word from the word bank to make two sentences into one. A word can be used more than once.

Word Bank

and	but	for	nor	or	so	yet

1. Jack threw the leaves. Ann threw the leaves.

   Jack _____ Ann threw the leaves.

2. My brother played soccer. My brother played baseball.

   My brother played soccer _____ baseball.

3. I was tired. I didn't play.

   I was tired, _____ I didn't play.

4. Chu loves games. Walt doesn't love games.

   Chu loves games, _____ Walt doesn't love games.

Make One from Two
Combine the Sentences

Use the word bank to combine two sentences into one sentence.
A word can be used more than once.

> **Word Bank**
>
> and   but   for   nor   or   so   yet

1. The lion roared. The tiger roared.

    _____

2. The monkey jumped. The zebra didn't jump.

    _____

    _____

3. The elephant drank. The elephant ate.

    _____

4. The hippo was tired. The hippo slept.

    _____

    _____

Write Sentences
Write About the Picture

Write sentences about the picture using at least two joining words and two detail words from the word bank.

Detail Words			Joining Words			
on	in	through	and	but	for	
during	up	until	nor	or	so	yet
toward	after	into				

_____

_____

_____

_____

Write Sentences

Tell Me About My Sentences

Have another person read your sentences and answer the questions.

1. Are all the sentences about the picture?

    A. Yes   **B.** No

2. Does one sentence have a detail word?

    A. Yes   **B.** No

    Write the sentence.

    _____

3. Does one sentence have a joining word?

    A. Yes   **B.** No

    Write the sentence.

    _____

4. Does each sentence start with a capital letter and have an end mark?

    A. Yes   **B.** No

Statements and Commands

Make Sentences

Cut out the cards. Use them to make sentences.

WRITING SKILLS

ran up the clock.	went to the school.	The cow
Humpty Dumpty	jumped on a bus.	jumped over the moon.
sat on a wall.	The frog	A mouse

Statements and Commands
Tell Something and Give Orders

▶ A **statement** tells something.
It ends with a period.

Jane wants to dance. ← period

▶ A **command** gives an order.
It usually ends with a period

Dance with me. ← period

Read the sentence. Write *S* next to the statements. Write *C* next to the commands.

1. Jane does the hokey pokey. ____

2. Do the hokey pokey with Jane. ____

3. Jane plans a party. ____

4. Come to Jane's party. ____

Statements and Commands
Recognize and Write Statements and Commands

Add a capital letter and a period to the sentence.

1. ___ ohnny plays with Max ___

2. ___ it, Max ___

Write one statement about Max.

3. _____

Write one command that Johnny might say to Max.

4. _____

✦ Reward

Questions

Want to Learn About Questions?

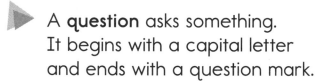

▶ A **question** asks something. It begins with a capital letter and ends with a question mark.

Who likes animals?

↑ capital letter   ↑ question mark

Read the sentence. Write *Yes* if the sentence is a question. Write *No* if it is not.

1. Can you hop like a frog? _____

2. Count to ten. _____

3. Can you bark like a dog? _____

4. Well, do it, then. _____

Questions

Recognize and Write Questions

Write a question mark at the end of a question. Write a period at the end of a statement.

1. Do you like pizza ____

2. What should we put on top ____

3. I want ham on mine ____

Write one question about pizza.

4. _____

_____

Exclamations

Wow! Show Strong Feelings

▶ An **exclamation** shows strong feeling. It ends with an exclamation mark.

Bumper cars are so much fun! ← exclamation mark

Make a check (✓) if the sentence is an exclamation.

1. Is it raining? ____

2. The ball is round. ____

3. I love baseball! ____

4. What time is it? ____

5. That was fun! ____

Exclamations

Punctuate and Write Exclamations

Use the words in the word bank to finish the exclamation.
Add an exclamation mark.

Word Bank

| step | Jeff | snake | cold |

1. Your _____ is really long ___

2. It feels very _____

3. Don't _____ on my pet ___

4. _____ doesn't want to hold it ___

Write one exclamation about a snake.

5. _____

Follow Directions

Add a Step

Listen to the steps and do them in order: first Step 1; then Steps 1 and 2; then Steps 1, 2, and 3; and so on.

1. Touch your toes.

2. Jump in the air.

3. Turn in a circle.

4. Sit on the floor.

5. Do five jumping jacks.

6. Spread your arms wide.

7. Clap three times.

8. Hop like a frog.

Follow Directions
Use Directions

Cut out the sentences. Place them in order to explain how to brush your teeth. On the blank strip, add a step that you think is missing.

Open your mouth.

Get your toothbrush.

Brush your bottom teeth.

Brush your top teeth.

Rinse out your mouth.

_____

WRITING SKILLS

Follow Directions

Make a Cartoon Dog

On a sheet of paper, follow the steps to draw a cartoon dog.

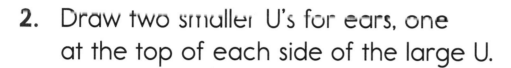

1. Draw a large capital U.

2. Draw two smaller U's for ears, one at the top of each side of the large U.

3. Connect the top of the large U to make the head.

4. Draw two small circles with a dot inside each circle for the eyes.

5. Draw a small circle for the nose. Color it in.

6. Add one more U for the tongue. Draw a line down the middle of the tongue.

WRITING SKILLS

Put Steps in Order
Story Order

Cut out the cards, and then put them in order.

Put Steps in Order
Order Words

Choose the word that connects each event, or step, to the next one.

1. _____, we climbed in the car.

   A. First   **C.** Next

   B. Then   **D.** Finally

2. _____, we put on our seatbelts.

   A. First   **C.** Next

   B. Then   **D.** Finally

3. _____, Mom drove to the highway.

   A. First   **C.** Next

   B. Then   **D.** Finally

4. _____, we sang songs in the car.

   A. First   **C.** Next

   B. Then   **D.** Finally

5. _____, we arrived at the park!

   A. First   **C.** Next

   B. Then   **D.** Finally

Put Steps in Order
Use Order Words

Complete the story by adding the correct order word to the sentence.

Word Bank

next   first   finally   then

Rita is washing her dog.

1. _____, she puts water in the tub.

2. _____, she adds soap to the water.

3. _____, she puts her dog in the tub.

4. _____, she washes her dog.

5. _____, Rita pulls her dog out of the tub and dries him off.

Learn

Plan the Steps

Graphic Organizer

Fill in the graphic organizer with the steps for your activity.

Step 1

↓

Step 2

↓

Step 3

↓

Step 4

WRITING SKILLS

Write the Steps

Review Sentences and Order Words

Read the sentence, and write what is wrong with it.

1. First, we played   _____

2. Then, I   _____

3. Next, went on the slide.   _____

4. finally, we went home.   _____

Write the Steps
Write a How-To

Write four sentences that tell how to do something. If you have more than four steps, write more sentences. Use the order words *first*, *next*, *then*, and *finally*.

_____

_____

_____

_____

_____

_____

_____

LANGUAGE ARTS GREEN

Write the Steps
Tell Me About My How-To

Have another person read your how-to and answer the questions.

1. Do all the steps explain how to do something?

    A. Yes　　　　　　　　　**B.** No

2. Does each sentence begin with an order word?

    A. Yes　　　　　　　　　**B.** No

3. Does the first sentence begin with the word *First*?

    A. Yes　　　　　　　　　**B.** No

4. Does the last sentence begin with the word *Finally*?

    A. Yes　　　　　　　　　**B.** No

5. Could you follow these steps to do the activity described?

    A. Yes　　　　　　　　　**B.** No

6. Write any sentence that is missing an order word.

_____

_____

_____

Common Nouns

Find the Nouns

 A **noun** names a person, place, or thing.

My friend threw a ball in the park.

↑   ↑   ↑

person   **thing**   **place**

WRITING SKILLS

Circle the noun in the sentence. Write whether it is a person, place, or thing.

1. My uncle smiled. _____

2. The car was shiny. _____

3. My bedroom is dirty. _____

4. We tossed a baseball. _____

5. I visited a farm. _____

Common Nouns

Use Nouns

Use the word bank to fill in the blank in the sentence. Each sentence is missing a person, place, or thing.

Person	Place	Thing
sister	beach	cupcake
friend	house	yo-yo
dad	farm	jacket

1. My _____ read me a story.

2. I bought a _____.

3. Liz walked to the _____.

4. Carl held a _____ in his hands.

5. I gave a present to my _____.

WRITING SKILLS

Proper Nouns

Noun Scavenger Hunt

Go on a scavenger hunt for nouns. Find at least three nouns for each column.

Person	Place	Thing

WRITING SKILLS

Proper Nouns
Common and Proper Nouns

▶ A **proper noun** names a specific person, place, or thing. It begins with a capital letter.

Common Noun	Proper Noun
boy	Robbie
city	Boston
day	Monday

Read the sentence. Write *P* above the proper noun and *C* above the common noun in the sentence.

1. Our dog Rex is digging.

2. We are traveling in the month of June.

3. My cousin Alice is visiting.

4. I am studying the country Russia.

5. His favorite book is *Dinosaurs*!

Proper Nouns
Capitalize Proper Nouns

Fix the sentence. Use a capital letter to begin the proper noun.
The first one has been done for you.

1. My mom's name is D̸ebbie.

2. I'm going swimming on monday.

3. My brother jim is late.

4. My sister kate takes dance lessons.

Write a proper noun in the blank.

5. My birthday is in the month of _____.

6. The name of my best friend is _____.

Possessive Nouns

Find Possessives

▶ A **possessive noun** shows that a person or animal has or owns something. Use an apostrophe and *s* to make a noun possessive.

The puppy belongs to Ann.
Ann's puppy is small.

↑
possessive noun

Circle the possessive noun in the sentence.

1. I put food in the rabbit's cage.

2. Buzz is my brother's rabbit.

3. Carrots are Buzz's favorite food.

4. My sister's pet is a hamster.

5. The hamster's name is Cleo.

Possessive Nouns
Use Possessives

Choose the correct possessive noun for the sentence.

1. I am playing with _____ cars.

   A. Ryan   **B.** Ryan's   **C.** Ryans

2. He is cleaning his _____ cage.

   A. turtle's   **B.** turtles   **C.** turtle

Use the correct possessive noun in the sentence.

3. The dog has a bone. It is the _____ bone.

4. My sister has a baseball. It is my _____ baseball.

5. Chu has a hat. That is _____ hat.

WRITING SKILLS

Find Facts

Explore Your Topic

Read the article on the topic you chose. Look for facts.

George Washington

George Washington was born in 1732 in the Virginia colony. He did well in school. George became a surveyor. Then, he joined the Virginia army. England was at war with France. Because England owned Virginia, George fought for England in the war. He became famous for being brave. In 1759, George married a woman named Martha. The American Revolution began. George became the general of America's army. George Washington was a great general. He helped America win the war. In 1789, he became America's first president. He served as president for eight years. George Washington died in 1799.

Women in Space

Americans went to space in 1961. At first, there were no women astronauts. In 1978, six women became astronauts. One of those women was Sally Ride. Sally Ride was interested in science. In 1983, she went into space on the space shuttle. She was the first American woman in space. In 1984, another woman went into space. Her name was Kathryn Sullivan. She was the first American woman to walk in space. Mae Jemison was an African American woman. She became the first African American female astronaut. Ellen Ochoa learned about Sally Ride. She saw that women could go into space. Ellen Ochoa went into space four times. More than 50 women have gone into space.

Try It

Find Facts

Pick Your Facts

Find five or six facts you want to write about. Write each fact on a line.

Topic ______________________________

1. ______________________________

____

2. ______________________________

____

3. ______________________________

____

4. ______________________________

____

WRITING SKILLS

5. _____

_____

6. _____

_____

Write in Your Own Words
Find Your Own Words

Look at some ways that the same information can be rewritten. Then, rewrite the information in your own way.

> In 1983, Sally Ride became the first American woman to go into space.

Example 1: Sally Ride was the first American woman astronaut.

Example 2: Before Sally Ride, no American woman had ever gone into space.

Example 3: An interesting fact about Sally Ride is that she was the first American female astronaut.

1. _____

_____

_____

_____

2. _____

_____

_____

_____

_____

Write in Your Own Words
Rewrite the Facts

Rewrite the information that you researched in your own way.

1. The most important fact about my topic is

    _____

    _____.

2. What I find most interesting about my topic is

    _____

    _____.

3. Did you know that _____

    _____ ?

4. _____

    _____

5. _____

_____

6. _____

_____

Create a Fact Cube
Write a Fact Cube

Write your facts on the cube. Draw a picture that goes with your facts. Cut out the shape, and fold along the lines. Glue or tape the tabs.

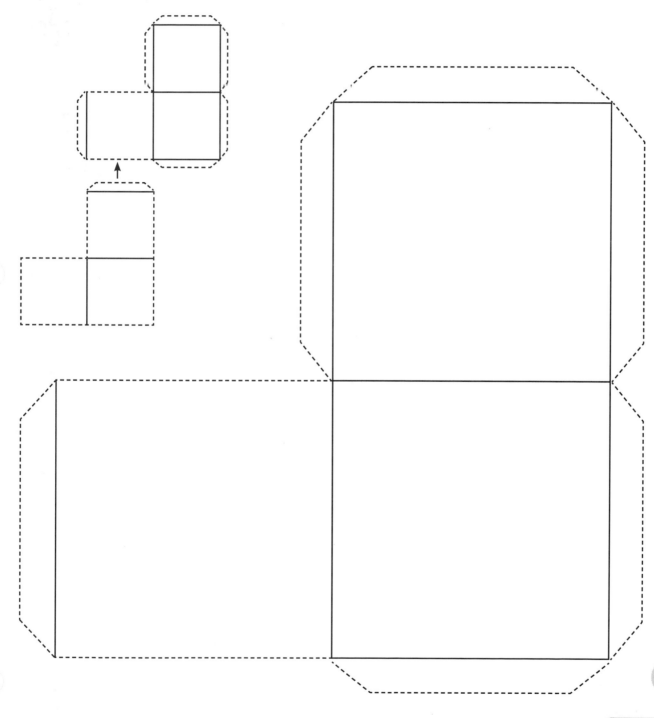

Create a Fact Cube
Tell Me About My Fact Cube

Have another person read your fact cube and answer the questions.

1. Are there at least five sentences on the cube and one picture?

   A. Yes　　　　　　　　　**B.** No

2. Does any sentence seem like an opinion instead of a fact?

   A. Yes　　　　　　　　　**B.** No

   Write the sentence.

   _____

3. Are the facts in an order that makes sense?

   A. Yes　　　　　　　　　**B.** No

4. Does each sentence start with a capital letter and have an end mark?

   A. Yes　　　　　　　　　**B.** No

WRITING SKILLS

Action Verbs

Find Action Verbs

▶ A **verb** is a word that shows action.

We play outside.

↑
verb

Circle the action verb in the sentence.

1. We hike on the trail.

2. My brother picks flowers.

3. Our friends swim in the lake.

4. We smile at each other.

Action Verbs
Use Action Verbs

Circle the action verb in the sentence.

1. I love pancakes with maple syrup.

2. Eat these pancakes with me.

Use a word from the word bank to complete the sentence.

> **Word Bank**
>
> go   read   play
> run   jump

3. Let's _____ to the store.

4. I always _____ books after school.

5. _____ on the trampoline.

Verbs with Nouns
Act Out Verbs

Cut out the cards. Do the action on each card.

I sit on the floor.

I sing a loud note.

I think about ice cream.

Verbs with Nouns

Singular Verbs and Singular Nouns

A **noun** and a **verb** must fit together.
If the noun is **singular**, the verb must be **singular**.

The cow moos.

singular singular
noun   verb

Choose the sentence in which the noun and verb fit together.

1. Which sentence is correct?

   A. My cat meow.

   B. My cats meows.

   C. My cat meows.

2. Which sentence is correct?

   A. The flower smell nice.

   B. The flower smells nice.

   C. The flowers smells nice.

3. Which sentence is correct?

   A. The trucks honks.

   B. The truck honks.

   C. The truck honk.

4. Which sentence is correct?

   A. The boy sleep on the couch.

   B. The boys sleeps on the couch.

   C. The boy sleeps on the couch.

Verbs with Nouns
Use Singular Verbs

Circle the correct verb.

1. The rain (fall,   falls) from the sky.

2. The sun (shine,   shines) on our faces.

3. My mother (look,   looks) at the clouds.

Write a verb that fits with the noun to complete the sentence.

4. The ball _____ down the hill.

5. The wolf _____ at the moon.

More Verbs with Nouns
Plural Verbs and Plural Nouns

▶ A **noun** and a **verb** must fit together.
If the noun is **plural**, the verb must be **plural**.

The owls hoot.

plural   plural
noun   verb

Choose the sentence in which the noun and verb fit together.

1. Which sentence is correct?

    A. The players kicks the ball.

    B. The players kick the ball.

2. Which sentence is correct?

    A. Dick and Sally love soccer.

    B. Dick and Sally loves soccer.

3. Which sentence is correct?

    A. Both teams likes the game, too.

    B. Both teams like the game, too.

More Verbs with Nouns
Use Plural Verbs

Choose the correct word to complete the sentence, and write it on the line.

1. My brothers _____ the leaves.

   A. rake   **B.** rakes

2. My _____ weed the garden.

   A. sisters   **B.** sister

3. My friends _____ the garage.

   A. cleans   **B.** clean

Write two sentences using plural verbs from the word bank.

```
Word Bank
jump          dance          play          leap
```

4. _____

5. _____

Get Started with Your News
What Is News?

Cut out the cards, and then sort Alexander's sentences into *news* and *not news* piles.

Today, I woke up.

I won a checkers tournament!

The sun came up.

My family got a dog.

The dog's name is Max.

We ate dinner.

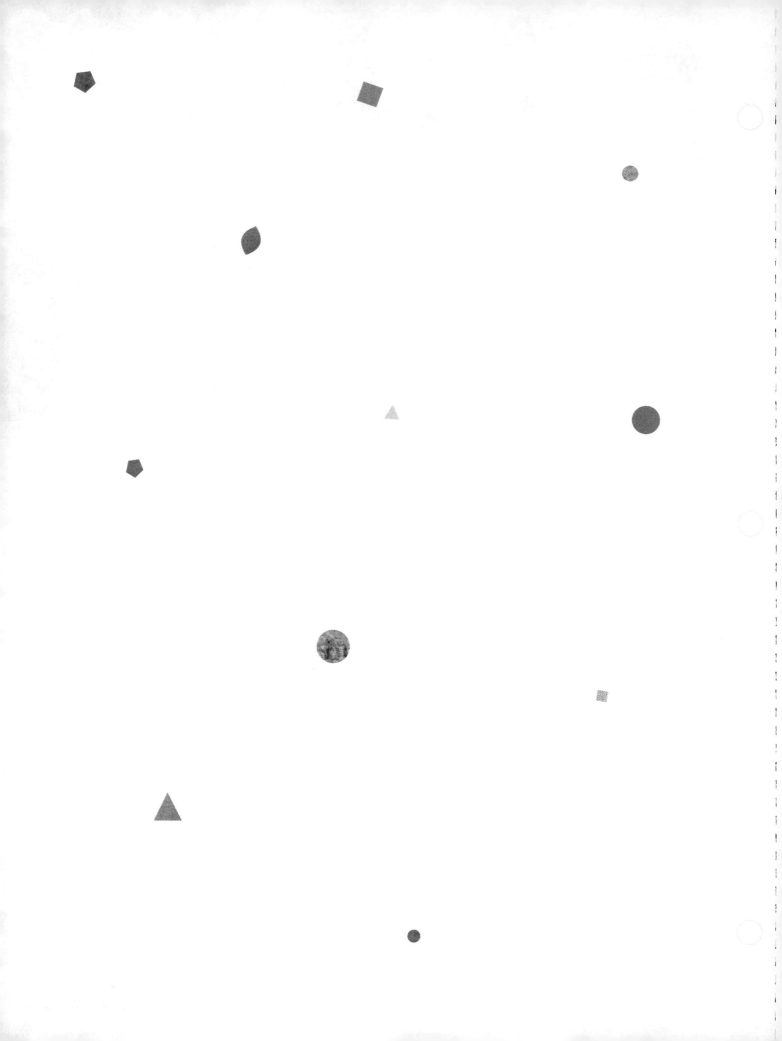

Friendly Letter Form
What Is a Friendly Letter?

Cut out and read the letter.

> July 20, 2012
>
> Dear Cousin Jack,
>
> I am writing to tell you some great news! I am going to be in the town play. I am going to play the part of the Train Conductor. I am the star of the show!
>
> I hope you can come see the play.
>
> Love,
> Alison

Friendly Letter Form
Follow the Form

Write the names of the parts of a friendly letter. Underline the capital letters in the date and greeting. Circle the commas.

July 20, 2012 → _____

Dear Cousin Jack, → _____

I am writing to tell you some great news! I am going to be in the town play. I am going to play the part of the Train Conductor. I am the star of the show!

I hope you can come see the play. →

Love, → _____

Alison → _____

Friendly Letter Form
Plan Your Letter

Fill in the blanks with information for the letter you plan to write.

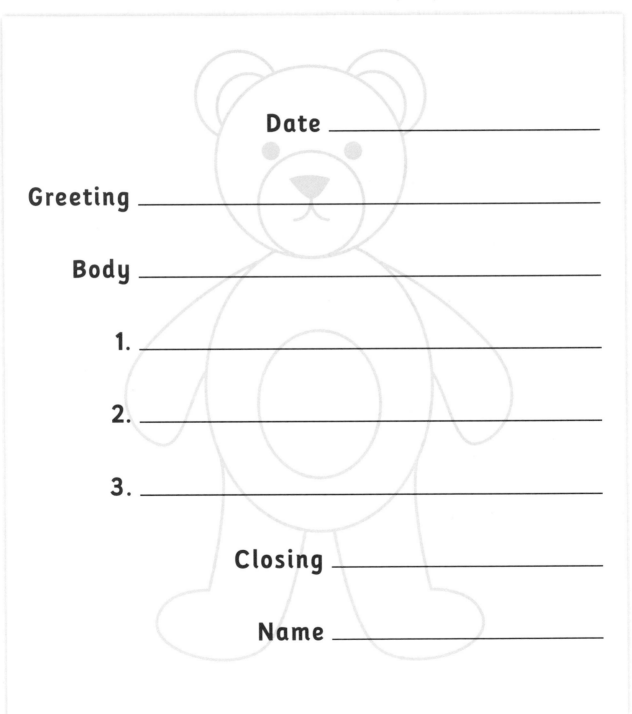

Date _____

Greeting _____

Body _____

1. _____

2. _____

3. _____

Closing _____

Name _____

Draft Your Letter

Write the Letter

Fill in the lines with the parts of your letter.

Date _____ _____

Greeting _____

Body _____

_____

_____

_____

Closing _____

Name _____

Address an Envelope
How Does the Mail Get Here?

Cut out the cards, and then hop from place to place, traveling the same path as a letter takes.

your house

your post office

your friend's post office

your friend's house

Address an Envelope

How to Address an Envelope

Look at each part of the envelope.

FOREVER USA

James Kent
4500 Crooked Tree Drive
Anchorage, AK 99516

Shawnee Price ← **name**
12 Red Rock Lane ← **street**
Mesa, AZ 85210
← ← ←
city state zip code

Write and Mail Your Letter
Publish and Mail Your Letter

Fill in the lines with the parts of your letter.

_____

_____

_____

_____

_____

_____

_____

WRITING SKILLS

Write and Mail Your Letter
Tell Me About My Letter

Have another person read your letter and answer the questions.

1. Does the letter tell about news?

   A. Yes   **B.** No

2. Does any part of the letter **not** tell news?

   A. Yes   **B.** No

   Write the sentence.

   _____

3. Is there a date, greeting, body, closing, and name?

   A. Yes   **B.** No

4. Which parts are missing?

   _____

5. Does each sentence start with a capital letter and have an end mark?

   A. Yes   **B.** No

Personal Pronouns

Find Personal Pronouns

▶ A **pronoun** is a word that takes the place of a noun.

<u>Lee</u> likes salad.

⬆

(He) eats vegetables every day.

▶ The **pronoun** *I* is always capitalized.

<u>Lee</u> said (I) should try some peas.

Circle the pronoun in the second sentence that replaces the underlined noun in the first sentence.

1. <u>Ryan</u> laughs. (He,   It,   You) loves jokes.

2. <u>Ali</u> had my ball. (I,   She,   You) gave it back to me.

3. There's <u>Melissa</u>. Let's talk to (I,   her,   you).

4. My <u>room</u> is dirty. (He,   She,   It) needs to be cleaned.

Personal Pronouns
Use Personal Pronouns

Use a pronoun from the word bank in the blank in the second sentence. The pronoun should replace the underlined noun or nouns in the first sentence.

Word Bank		
her	it	we
you	he	me

1. <u>Carl</u> is tired. _____ was up late.

2. <u>Ellen</u> pulls the cart. Rico helps _____.

3. <u>Bree and I</u> read books. _____ love reading.

Write the pronoun *I* correctly in the sentence.

4. It's late, so i am going to sleep.

5. You and i should see the circus!

Possessive Pronouns
Review Possessive Nouns

Cut out the cards, and use them to make phrases with a possessive noun.

the	's	dog
car	cow	hippo
hat	slide	tuba

Possessive Pronouns

Find Possessive Pronouns

▶ A **possessive pronoun** has or owns something.
It takes the place of a possessive noun.

possessive noun

Margo is reading <u>Margo's</u> new book.

Margo is reading (her) new book.

possessive pronoun

Circle the possessive pronoun in the sentence.

1. The lion is feeding its cubs.

2. Lena is showing me her picture.

3. I am working on my art.

4. My brothers are riding their bikes.

5. Did you write your name on the paper?

Possessive Pronouns
Use Possessive Pronouns

Circle the possessive pronoun in the sentence.

1. My mom is on TV!

2. Do you like our band?

Use a possessive pronoun from the word bank in the sentence. The possessive pronoun should match the underlined word or words.

Word Bank

my	your	her
his	its	their

3. <u>Helen</u> dropped _____ pencil.

4. Wait! <u>You</u> forgot _____ coat.

5. I can't use <u>this computer</u> because _____ keys are broken.

Indefinite Pronouns
Review Pronouns

Match the noun with its pronoun.

Jane	his
Mark's	its
Tim and Eric	she
the chair's	them

WRITING SKILLS

Indefinite Pronouns
Find Indefinite Pronouns

▶ Some pronouns replace nouns that haven't been named.

(**Everyone**) **is at the beach.**

• •

Circle the pronoun in the sentence.

1. Has anyone seen Jack's bag?

2. Somebody ate the cookies!

3. Most of the cows are brown.

4. Nobody else was at the park today.

5. The leader gave prizes to all.

Indefinite Pronouns
Use Indefinite Pronouns

Use a pronoun from the word bank to make the sentence describe its picture.

> **Word Bank**
>
> Nobody   Everyone   Someone

1. _____ is at dinner.

2. _____ is in the garage.

3. _____ is hiding.

Write a sentence using the pronoun *anyone*.

4. _____

   _____

Opinions and Paragraphs
Support an Opinion

Read the opinion and the reasons for that opinion. Write two more reasons.

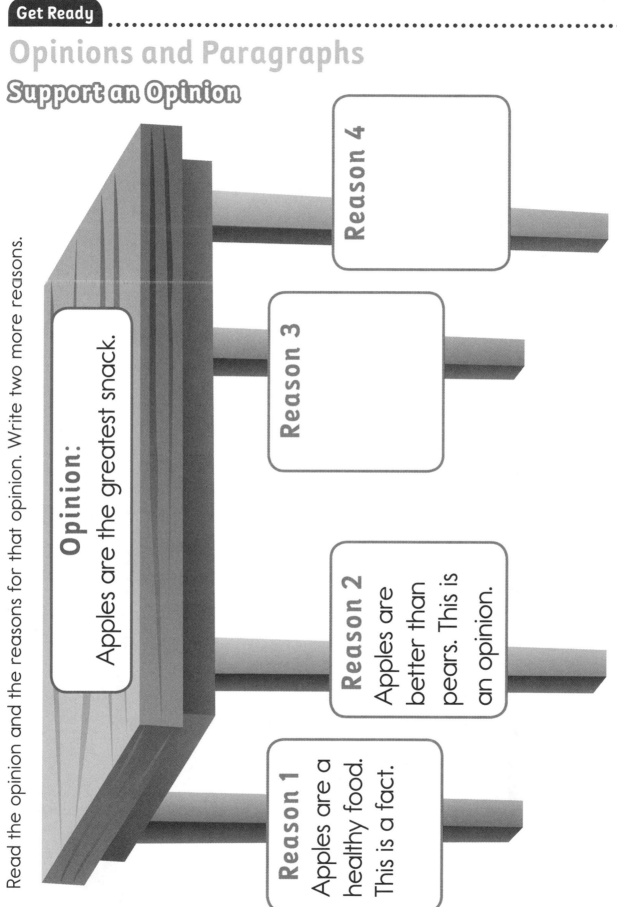

Opinion:
Apples are the greatest snack.

Reason 1
Apples are a healthy food. This is a fact.

Reason 2
Apples are better than pears. This is an opinion.

Reason 3

Reason 4

Opinions and Paragraphs
What Is a Paragraph?

Find your way through the maze by following the ideas that are related to the picture on Story Card F. Cross out sentences that are **not** related to the topic or picture on the story card.

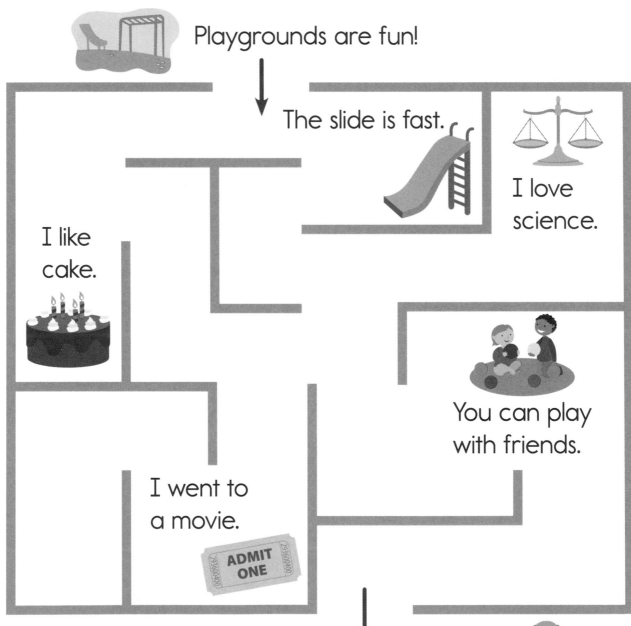

Playgrounds are fun!

The slide is fast.

I love science.

I like cake.

You can play with friends.

I went to a movie.

ADMIT ONE

Dogs can come, too!

Opinions and Paragraphs
Find Supporting Sentences

Read the paragraph. Look for the sentences that are related. Cross out the sentences that do **not** relate to the first sentence.

The circus is a lot of fun! The circus is filled with interesting animals. There are animals at the zoo. You can see acrobats who do cool tricks. There are funny clowns who make jokes. My brother is funny. I share a room with my brother. I love the circus because it is exciting.

WRITING SKILLS

State an Opinion
Use Transitions

WRITING SKILLS

▶ Use **transition words** to connect a reason to an opinion.

because

I love soccer. It is fun.

Circle the transition word.

1. I love the piano because I can use it to make music.

2. I don't need a band to play, so I can play by myself.

3. Also, people can sing along when I play.

4. I like the way a piano sounds, and that's why I love playing the piano.

State an Opinion

Use a Graphic Organizer

Add your opinion and reasons to the graphic organizer. Write transition words on the connecting lines.

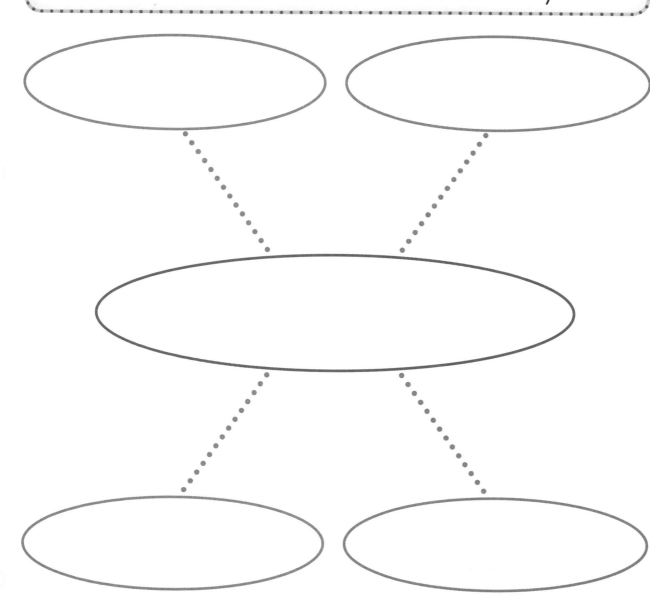

Word Bank

also	so	therefore
because	too	and that's why

Write Your Opinion
Draft Your Opinion Paragraph

Write your opinion paragraph. Write in complete sentences.

Opinion: _____

_____

Reasons: _____

_____

_____

_____

_____

Conclusion: _____

_____

Publish Your Opinion
Review the Checklist

Answer the questions to help revise your opinion paragraph.

1. Does your first sentence tell your opinion?

   A. Yes   **B.** No

2. Do all of the sentences tell reasons for your opinion?

   A. Yes   **B.** No

3. Are some of the sentences facts?

   A. Yes   **B.** No

4. Do you use transition words such as *because, so, also*, and *as well* to connect your ideas?

   A. Yes   **B.** No

5. Do you use strong words to describe your feelings?

   A. Yes   **B.** No

WRITING SKILLS

6. Does your last sentence tell your opinion again in a new way?

   A. Yes   **B.** No

7. Does every sentence have a naming part and an action part?

   A. Yes   **B.** No

8. Does every sentence begin with a capital letter and end with an end mark?

   A. Yes   **B.** No

Publish Your Opinion

Publish Your Opinion Paragraph

Write the final draft of your opinion paragraph.

_____

_____

_____

_____

_____

_____

_____

_____

_____

WRITING SKILLS

_____

_____

_____

_____

_____

 Reward . . . .

Draw a picture to show your opinion.

Peer Interaction

Publish Your Opinion

Tell Me About My Opinion Paragraph

Have another person read your opinion paragraph and answer these questions.

1. Does the paragraph state an opinion?

   A. Yes **B.** No

2. What is the writer's opinion?

   ____

   ____

3. Do middle sentences give reasons for the opinion?

   A. Yes **B.** No

4. Are all the reasons connected to the opinion?

   A. Yes **B.** No

WRITING SKILLS

If **not**, tell which sentence or reason isn't.

_____

_____

5. Is there a final sentence that repeats the opinion in different words or ends the paragraph?

   A. Yes   **B.** No

6. Does each sentence start with a capital letter and have an end mark?

   A. Yes   **B.** No

Present Tense

Understand Present Tense Verbs

▶ A **present tense verb** tells about present time. The verb shows an action that is a habit or happens repeatedly.

I <u>eat</u> ice cream.

↑
present tense

Circle the verb that tells about present time.

1. Joe beats the drum.

2. We play on the soccer field.

3. I sing on the stage.

4. She pushes the swing.

Present Tense

Use Present Tense Verbs

Use a present tense verb from the word bank to complete the sentence.

> ### Word Bank
> sleep   listens   wake   dreams   falls

1. Cara _____ to music before bed.

2. The rain _____ on the roof.

3. Cara and her dog _____ .

4. Cara _____ about friends.

5. They _____ up to a sunny day.

Past Tense
What's Happening Now?

Act out the verb on the card.

jump	stand
sing	sit
wiggle	stretch
clap	hop

Past Tense

Understand Past Tense Verbs

▶ A **past tense verb** tells about past time. The verb shows action that has already happened.

Yesterday, I <u>cleaned</u> my room.

↑
past tense

Circle the verb that tells about past time.

1. My uncle played the guitar.

2. My cousins danced.

3. Dad cooked lunch.

4. I climbed a tree.

WRITING SKILLS

Past Tense

Use Past Tense Verbs

Find the correct verb in the word bank to fill in the blank. Add *–d* or *–ed* to make it a past tense verb.

> ### Word Bank
> smile   walk   watch   laugh

1. Yesterday, my friends and I _____ a movie.

2. I _____ the whole time.

3. I _____ out loud at the funny parts.

4. After the movie, we _____ home.

Future Tense Verbs

Understand Future Tense Verbs

▶ A **future tense verb** tells about future time. The verb shows action that will happen later.

Tomorrow, I will swim in the lake.

↑
future tense

Circle the verb that tells about future time.

1. Later, we will play a game.

2. My sister will get a ball.

3. I will hide the ball in the house.

4. Everyone will look for the ball.

5. Someone will find the ball.

Future Tense

Use Future Tense Verbs

Rewrite the sentence. Change the verb to future tense. The first one has been done for you.

1. Right now, I eat breakfast.

   Tomorrow, **I will eat breakfast.**_____.

2. Today, I ride my bike.

   Tomorrow, _____.

3. I sit on the bench now.

   Later, _____.

4. Now, I read a book.

   Next week, _____.

5. Yesterday, I played on the slide.

   Tomorrow, _____.

Discover and Research Your Heritage
Research Your Heritage

Use an encyclopedia to answer the questions about your heritage.

1. The place I am writing about is _____

   _____ .

2. What is life like for children there? _____

   _____

3. What kinds of animals live there? _____

   _____

4. What kinds of games are played there? _____

   _____

5. What is the weather like there? _____

   _____

6. What are schools like for children? _____

_____

7. Two facts that I find interesting:

Fact 1 _____

_____

Fact 2 _____

_____

Write a Draft About Your Heritage
Write Your Draft

Write your paragraph about your heritage. Make sure you have an introduction and a conclusion. Include three to five facts in the body. Use words from the word bank to connect your sentences and ideas.

Word Bank			
first	next	then	and that's why
finally	also	too	because

_____

_____ **Introduction**

_____

_____

_____

_____ **Body**

_____

_____

_____

_____

_____

_____ } **Body**

_____

_____

_____

_____ } **Conclusion**

_____

_____

Revise Your Draft and Create a Visual Aid
Create Your Visual Aid

Create a visual aid about your topic. Answer the questions about your visual aid. Draw or paste your visual aid on the next page.

1. What is your visual aid?

   _____

   _____

   _____

   _____

2. How does your visual aid relate to your topic?

   _____

   _____

   _____

   _____

3. Draw your visual aid.

Revise Your Draft and Create a Visual Aid
Tell Me About My Heritage Paragraph

Have another person read your writing and answer these questions.

1. What place is the student writing about?

    _____

2. What is one interesting fact about that place?

    _____

    _____

3. Did the student use transitions?

    A. Yes   **B.** No

4. Is there a sentence that needs a transition?

    A. Yes   **B.** No

    Write the sentence.

    _____

5. Is there an introduction or hello sentence?

   A. Yes   **B.** No

Write the sentence.

_____

_____

6. Is there a conclusion or good-bye sentence?

   A. Yes   **B.** No

Write the sentence.

_____

_____

Share Your Heritage
Check Your Work

Answer the questions about your heritage paragraph.

1. Do you have a hello sentence to tell what your heritage paragraph is about?

    A. Yes   **B.** No

2. Do you have three to five facts about the place in your heritage paragraph?

    A. Yes   **B.** No

3. Do you have a good-bye sentence?

    A. Yes   **B.** No

4. Do you have order words and connecting words?

    A. Yes   **B.** No

5. Can you add a sentence to explain more about a fact?

    A. Yes   **B.** No

6. Are there details missing from your heritage paragraph?

   A. Yes   **B.** No

7. Did you create a visual aid to go with your heritage paragraph?

   A. Yes   **B.** No

Share Your Heritage

Present Your Heritage Paragraph

Write the final copy of your heritage paragraph.

_____

_____

_____

_____

_____

_____

_____

_____

WRITING SKILLS

_____

_____

_____

_____

_____

_____

_____

_____

_____

_____

Describing Words
Understand Adjectives

▶ An **adjective** describes a **noun**.

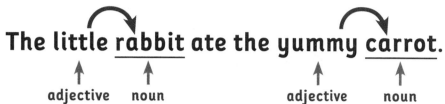

The little <u>rabbit</u> ate the yummy <u>carrot</u>.

adjective　noun　　　　adjective　noun

• •

Underline the adjective or adjectives in the sentence.

1. We went on the big slide.

2. I ate pink ice cream.

3. The kind man fixed the old bike.

4. The tiny bird sat on top of the red barn.

LANGUAGE ARTS GREEN　　**WS 131**

Describing Words
Use Descriptive Adjectives

Rewrite the sentence. Use adjectives from the word bank to describe the picture.

Word Bank
blue   green   tiny   white   red   giant

1. The frog looked up at the cow.

_____

_____

2. The leaves fell on the grass.

_____

_____

3. The sky has clouds.

_____

Articles

Understand Articles

▶ *The*, *a*, and *an* are articles.
Use *a* before a word that begins with a consonant.
Use *an* before a word that begins with a vowel sound.

The animals were very funny.

A book fell on the floor.

An elephant picked it up.

Circle the article or articles in the sentence.

1. The band played.

2. I gave my brother an orange.

3. A bug chewed on a leaf.

4. The cart lost a wheel.

Articles

Use Articles

Fill in the blank with the correct article. The first one has been done for you.

1. I want _____a_____ snack before bed.

    I'll eat _____the_____ apple left over from lunch.

2. There is _____ movie we should see.

    _____ movie is about a talking dog.

3. My brother bought _____ ant farm.

    He watches _____ ants all day.

Use the correct article *a* or *an* before the noun.

4. _____ monkey

5. _____ frog

6. _____ umbrella

7. _____ cow

8. _____ orange

9. _____ eel

10. _____ desk

11. _____ owl

Demonstratives
Use a Lot of Description

Cut out the cards. Use the cards to make a descriptive sentence.

the	a
boy	banana
yellow	shy
ate	green
giant	smelly
good	hungry

LANGUAGE ARTS GREEN

Demonstratives

Understand Demonstratives

▶ *This* and *these* point out things that are nearby.

This pear is juicy.
These crackers are dry.

▶ *That* and *those* point out things that are farther away.

That cloud is big.
Those stars are bright.

Circle the adjectives *this*, *that*, *these*, and *those* in the sentence.

1. Those cars are really fast!

2. I want to go to that movie.

3. This key fits in that lock.

4. Where did all these zebras come from?

Demonstratives
Use Demonstratives

Look at the picture. Use the adjective that describes the picture.

Word Bank

| this | that | these | those |

1. _____ hill is huge.

2. I am going to eat _____ peas.

3. _____ dog is so friendly.

4. Look at _____ anthill.

5. Let's go talk to _____ people.

Stories with a Beginning, Middle, and End

Build a Story Sandwich

Cut out the shapes. Write the beginning, middle, and end of your story.

Beginning

Title _____

_____

_____

_____

_____

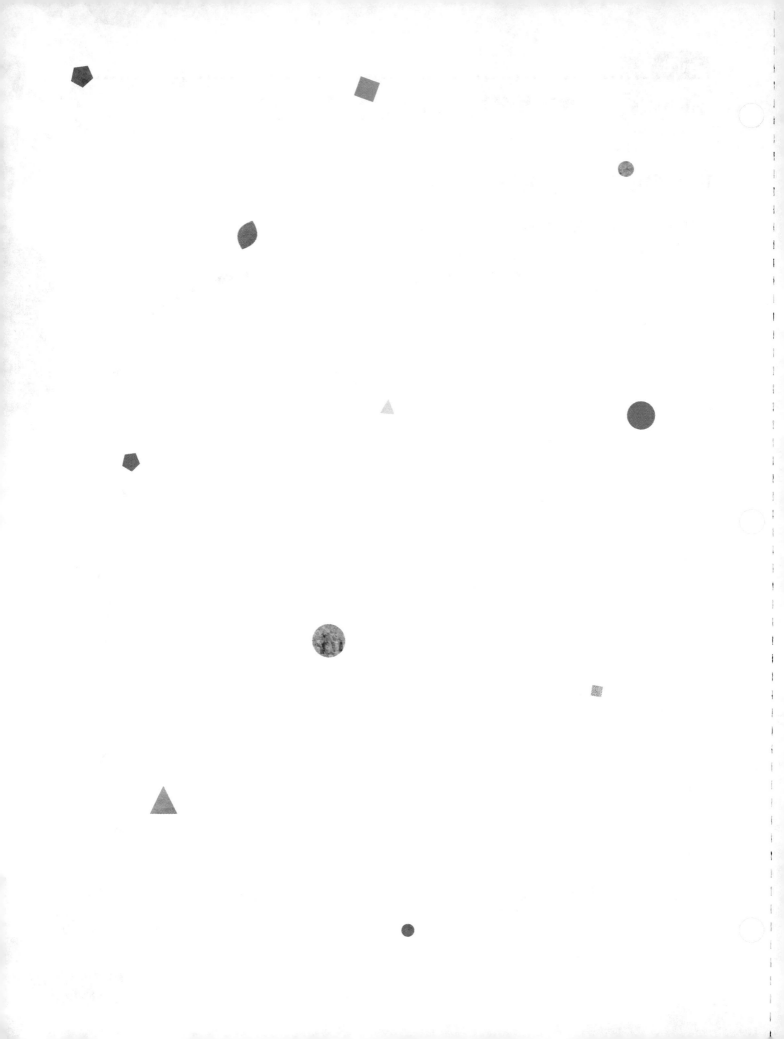

Middle

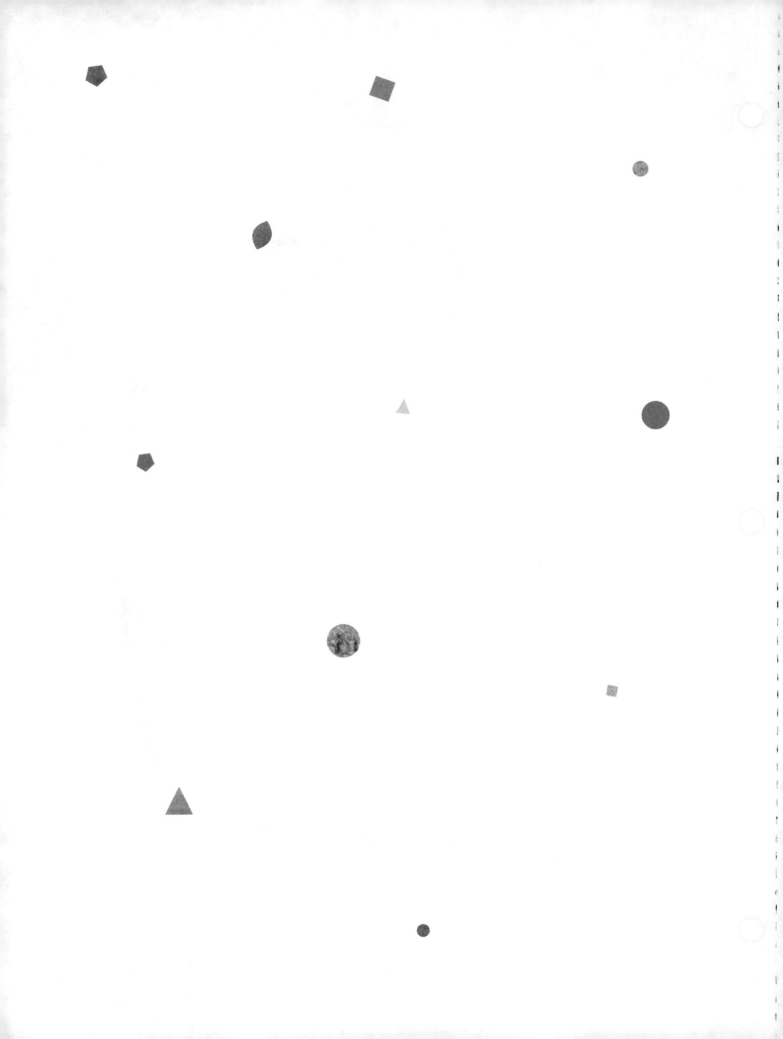

Middle

_____

_____

_____

_____

_____

_____

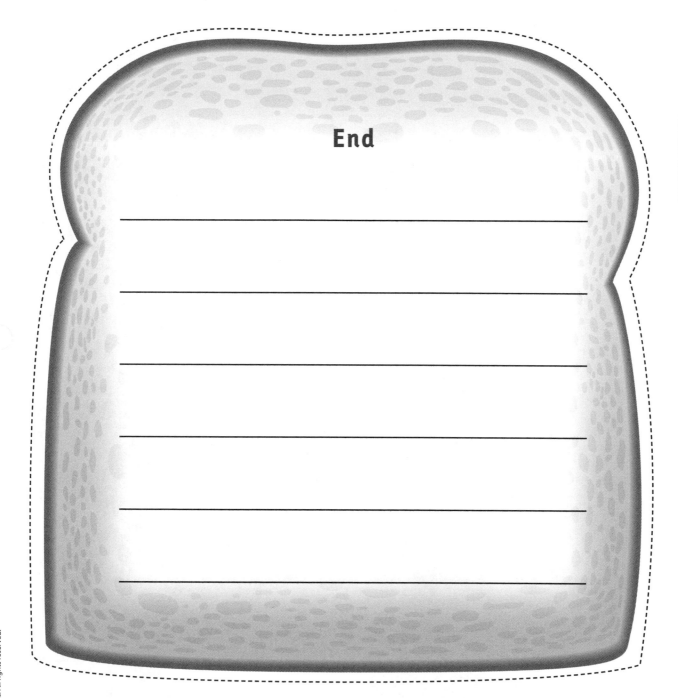

End

Add Strong Words
Tell Me More

Cut out the cards.

a shiny	**v** swallows
a giant	**v** chases
a greasy	**v** scares
a itchy	**v** paints
a crooked	**v** jumps

WRITING SKILLS

Add Strong Words
Write Strong Words

Cut out the shapes. Write strong verbs and adjectives.

Verbs

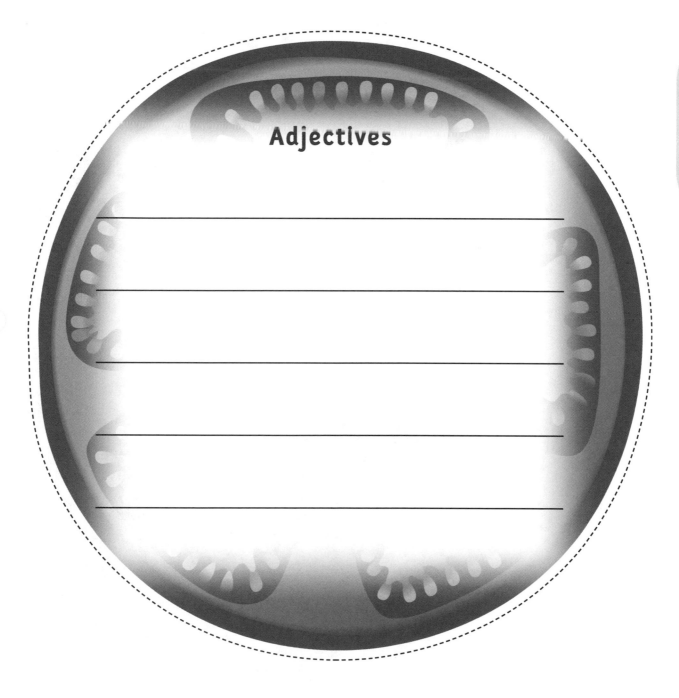

Adjectives

Write a Draft of Your Story
Time to Draft

Write your story. Include a beginning, middle, and end. Use order words as you write your draft. Order words are *first*, *next*, *then*, *last*, and *finally*.

_____

_____

_____

_____

_____

_____

_____

LANGUAGE ARTS GREEN

Write a Draft of Your Story
Tell Me About My Experience Story

Have another person read your experience story and answer these questions.

1. Is the story about a favorite day?

    A. Yes   **B.** No

2. Does the story have a beginning, middle, and end?

    A. Yes   **B.** No

3. If the story is missing a part, which part is missing?

    _____

    _____

    _____

4. Did the writer use order words and other transitions?

    A. Yes   **B.** No

5. What are some of the strong describing words or action words that helped you see the writer's story?

_____

_____

_____

6. Which detail from the story did you like best?

_____

_____

_____

Revise and Publish Your Experience Story

Check Your Work

Answer the questions about your experience story.

1. Does your story have a title?

   A. Yes   **B.** No

2. Does your story have a beginning, middle, and end?

   A. Yes   **B.** No

3. Does each sentence begin with a capital letter and end with an end mark?

   A. Yes   **B.** No

4. Are your sentences complete?

   A. Yes   **B.** No

5. Can you add details to your story?

   A. Yes   **B.** No

6. Can you add describing words?

   A. Yes   **B.** No

7. Can you add strong action words?

   A. Yes   **B.** No

LANGUAGE ARTS GREEN

Revise and Publish Your Experience Story
Publish Your Story

Write the final draft of your experience story, and draw an illustration.

_____

_____

_____

_____

_____

_____

_____

_____

WRITING SKILLS

_____

_____

_____

_____

_____

Contractions

Understand Contractions

▶ A **contraction** makes one word from two. Use an apostrophe in place of the missing letter.

Do not run in the hall.

(Don't) run in the hall.

↑

Do not = Don't

Read the pairs of sentences. Circle the contraction in the second sentence that replaces the underlined words in the first sentence.

1. I <u>could not</u> find my socks. I couldn't find my socks.

2. I <u>do not</u> want to be late. I don't want to be late.

3. There <u>is not</u> time to put on your socks! There isn't time to put on your socks!

4. We <u>have not</u> gone to this park before. We haven't gone to this park before.

Contractions

Use Contractions

Make a contraction from the pair of words. Then, use the contraction in a sentence.

1. had not = _____

_____

_____.

2. was not = _____

_____

_____.

3. did not = _____

_____

_____.

Words in a Series

Understand Words in a Series

▶ Use a **comma** between words in a series.

We played baseball, basketball, football, and soccer.

↑ comma   ↑ comma   ↑ comma

Add the missing comma in the sentence.

1. I have dogs, cats and lizards.

2. Pablo picked roses daisies, and lilacs.

3. The house was old, dark quiet, and scary.

4. We ran, jumped and skipped in the grass.

5. Ella washed rinsed, and dried the dishes.

Words in a Series

Use Words in a Series

Add the missing comma or commas to the sentence.

1. We listen to jazz, pop and classical music.

2. I collect worms, snails ladybugs and moths.

3. Everyone laughed cried cheered and clapped at the show.

Write a sentence that describes three things you like. For example, *I like bugs, plants, and rocks.*

4. _____

_____.

Dates

Review Proper Nouns

Cut out the cards. Match each common noun to its proper noun.

girl	Monday
day	Anne
city	Juan
month	Chicago
boy	April

Dates

Understand Dates

 The name of a month begins with a capital letter. A comma goes between the day and the year.

November 5, 1955

↑ capital letter   ↑ comma

NOVEMBER ❀

S	M	T	W	T	F	S
		1	2	3	4	5
6	7	8	9	10	11	12
13	14	15	16	17	18	19
20	21	22	23	24	25	26
27	28	29	30			

Look at the picture. Color the parts that have a correctly written date.

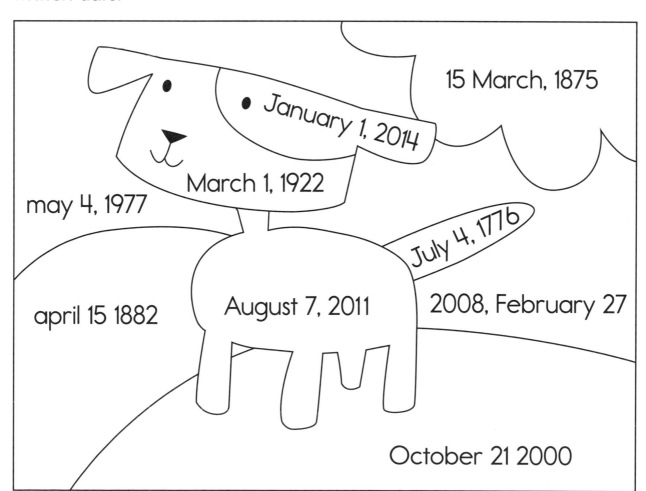

15 March, 1875

January 1, 2014

may 4, 1977

March 1, 1922

July 4, 1776

april 15 1882

August 7, 2011

2008, February 27

October 21 2000

Dates

Write Dates Correctly

Fix the date. The first one has been done for you.

S
1. ~~S~~eptember 11, 1901

2. may 22, 1991

3. January 14 2003

4. april 2 1966

5. July 22 2009

JULY 🌼						
S	**M**	**T**	**W**	**T**	**F**	**S**
			1	2	3	4
5	6	7	8	9	10	11
12	13	14	15	16	17	18
19	20	21	22	23	24	25
26	27	28	29	30	31	

Write the date when you were born.

6. _____

WRITING SKILLS

What Is a Book Report?
Read a Book Report

Read the book report.

My Report on <u>The Wizard of Oz</u>

I read the book <u>The Wizard of Oz</u> by L. Frank Baum. The illustrator is W.W. Denslow. The main characters are Dorothy, Toto, the Scarecrow, the Tin Man, the Cowardly Lion, Glinda, the Wizard, and the Wicked Witch. The setting for this book is in Oz.

First, Dorothy flies to Oz in her house. Then, she gets the slippers and wants to meet the wizard. Next, she meets three friends on the Yellow Brick Road. Then, she stops the Wicked Witch. Finally, the slippers take her home to Kansas.

I really liked this book because it was exciting. I thought the talking scarecrow and lion were cool. Also, I love stories about magic. <u>The Wizard of Oz</u> was a really great book.

What Is a Book Report?
Plan Your Book Report

Fill in the blanks with information about your book.

1. I read the book _____ .

2. The book is by _____ .

3. The book is illustrated by _____ .

4. The important characters in the book are _____

    _____

    _____

    _____ .

5. The setting of the book is _____

    _____

    _____ .

6. List three or four events that happen in the book.

First event: _____

_____

_____

Second event: _____

_____

_____

Third event: _____

_____

_____

Fourth event: _____

_____

7. List reasons why you like this book.

First reason: _____

_____

_____

Second reason: _____

_____

_____

Third reason: _____

_____

_____

Fourth reason: _____

_____

WRITING SKILLS

Write an Introduction and a Summary of Your Book

Write a Draft of Your Book Report

Fill in the information about your book to write the introduction to your book report.

Book report title: _____

I read the book _____

by _____.

The illustrator is _____.

The important main characters are _____

_____

_____.

The setting for this book is _____

_____.

Write a summary of the important events in your book. Use order words to tell the story.

Word Bank

first next then also finally

In this book, _____

_____

_____

_____

_____

_____

_____

LANGUAGE ARTS GREEN

Write a conclusion to your book report. State your opinion about the book. Tell your reasons. Use strong describing words.

I thought this book was _____,

because _____

_____

_____

_____

_____

_____

_____

Peer Interaction

Write an Opinion and Reasons

Tell Me About My Book Report

Have another person read your book report and answer these questions.

1. What book did the writer choose?

____

2. Who are the main characters?

____

____

3. What are the important events that happen in the book?

____

____

____

WRITING SKILLS

4. Did the writer use order words?

   A. Yes   **B.** No

5. Is there a sentence that needs an order word to connect it to the other sentences?

   A. Yes   **B.** No

6. Why did the writer like or not like the book?

_____

_____

_____

7. Does the writer make you want to read this book? Why or why not?

_____

_____

_____

Publish Your Book Report
Check Your Writing

Answer the questions about your book report.

1. Does your book report have a title?

   A. Yes   **B.** No

2. Did you include the book title, author, illustrator, setting, and characters?

   A. Yes   **B.** No

3. Does your summary include the important events in the book?

   A. Yes   **B.** No

4. Are the events in your summary in the order that they happen in the book?

   A. Yes   **B.** No

5. Do you use order words such as *first, next, then, also,* and *finally?*

   A. Yes   **B.** No

WRITING SKILLS

6. Did you write an opinion about your book?

A. Yes **B.** No

7. Do your reasons support your opinion?

A. Yes **B.** No

8. Are all your sentences complete sentences?

A. Yes **B.** No

9. Does every sentence begin with a capital letter and end with an end mark?

A. Yes **B.** No

Publish Your Book Report
Write Your Final Draft

Use this form to write a final draft of your book report.

Title: _____

Introduction: _____

_____

_____

_____

_____

_____

_____

_____

WRITING SKILLS

Summary: _____

_____

_____

_____

_____

_____

Conclusion: I thought this book was _____

_____

_____

Sentences, Nouns, and Verbs

Practice Makes Perfect

Draw one line under the naming part and two lines under the action part.

1. My brother ate lunch.

2. Everyone watched the movie.

Fix the sentence. Write a capital letter at the beginning of the sentence, and add an end mark at the end of the sentence.

3. they went to the lake

4. where are my shoes

Add an end mark to the sentence.

5. That is the best news _____

6. Print your name _____

Choose the word group that is a sentence.

7. Which choice is a sentence?

    A. The house across the street.

    B. The people cross the street.

Read the sentence. Choose what kind of sentence it is.

8. Go to bed, please.

  A. statement   **C.** question

  B. command   **D.** exclamation

9. Where is Alice?

  A. statement   **C.** question

  B. command   **D.** exclamation

10. That's hot!

  A. statement   **C.** question

  B. command   **D.** exclamation

11. I am very tired.

  A. statement   **C.** question

  B. command   **D.** exclamation

Circle all the nouns.

12. Carl and Tim went to the lake on Tuesday.

WRITING SKILLS

Choose the noun that needs a capital letter.

13. Jan went to the store with maria.

    A. went

    B. store

    C. maria

14. Rob and bill eat lunch.

    A. bill

    B. eat

    C. lunch

Choose a possessive noun to fill in the blank.

15. Have you seen the _____ bone?

    A. dog's

    B. dogs

Circle the verb in the sentence.

16. We ride our bikes.

17. They smiled.

18. I dance every day.

Choose the sentence that is written correctly.

19. Which sentence is correct?

   A. My brother climb.

   B. My brother climbs.

20. Which sentence is correct?

   A. The girls laughs.

   B. The girls laugh.

Pronouns, Verb Tense, Adjectives, Capital Letters, and Punctuation

Practice Makes Perfect

Circle the pronoun or pronouns in the sentence.

1. She and I walked to the store.

2. My bike was at his house.

3. Everybody was listening to the band.

Choose the best pronoun to replace the underlined word or words.

4. <u>Betsy</u> knows how to juggle.

   A. Her

   B. He

   C. She

5. The coach cheered for <u>the players</u>.

   A. him

   B. them

   C. you

Write each verb on the correct line.

6. Past Tense   **7.** Present Tense   **8.** Future Tense

_____   _____   _____

Choose the correct verb tense to fill in the blank.

9. Last night, we _____ music.

  A. play   **B.** played   **C.** will play

10. Tomorrow, my brother _____ the car.

  A. wash   **B.** washed   **C.** will wash

Choose the verb that tells about present time.

11. Right now, I _____ my teeth.

  A. brush   **B.** brushed   **C.** will brush

Circle the adjectives in the sentence.

12. Fast yellow bees landed on tiny flowers.

WRITING SKILLS

Choose an article to fill in the blank.

13. _____ horse was very fast.

    A. An

    B. The

14. I read _____ book.

    A. a

    B. an

Choose an adjective to fill in the blank.

15. Who is _____ person under the tree?

    A. those   **B.** these   **C.** that

16. I would like to eat _____ cherries.

    A. these   **B.** that   **C.** this

Make a contraction using the underlined words in the sentence.

17. Sue <u>is not</u> awake. _____

18. The fish <u>have not</u> been fed today. _____

Add the missing commas to the sentence.

19. I love pizza, chicken milk, grapes and cheese.

Write the date correctly.

20. january 3 2013 _____

Create a Story Map
What Is a Story Map?

Add the correct labels to the story map. Use the word bank to help you.

Word Bank

Title	Problem	Main Characters
Solution	Setting	Other Characters

_____
Peter Pan

_____
the Lost Boys, Michael,
John, Tiger Lily,
the pirates

_____
Neverland

_____
The pirates kidnap the
Lost Boys and the
Darling family.

_____
Peter, Wendy,
Captain Hook,
Tinkerbell

_____
Peter rescues everyone, and
the Darling family decides
to go home.

Create a Story Map
Use a Story Map

Fill in the story map with ideas for your own story.

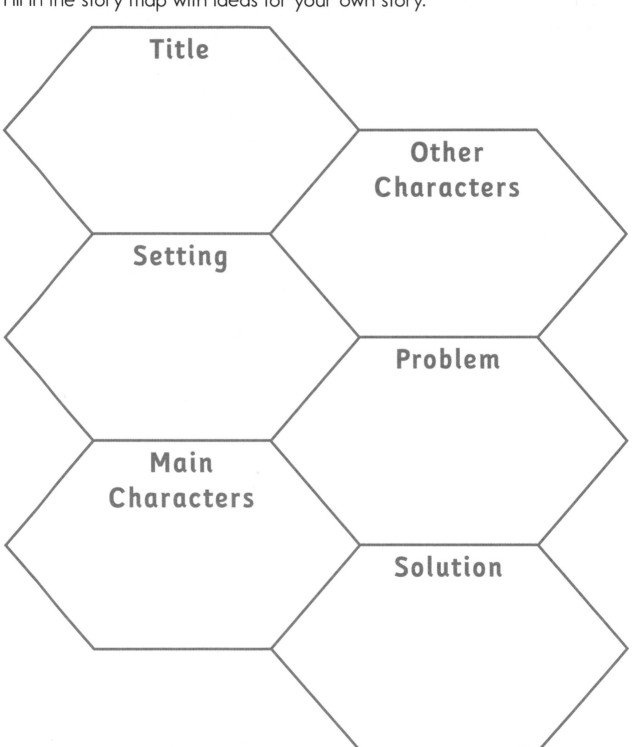

Title

Other Characters

Setting

Problem

Main Characters

Solution

Draft a Story
What Is Dialogue?

 Dialogue is the words that characters say. We can learn about characters from what they say.

Without dialogue: Jack loved all kinds of games.

With dialogue: "I love baseball, and playing robots, and building rockets to the moon!" said Jack. "I'll play anything fun!"

Rewrite the sentence. Write what the character says to tell the same ideas.

Without dialogue: Aya liked some animals, but she was afraid of others.

With dialogue: Aya said, "_____

_____

_____

_____."

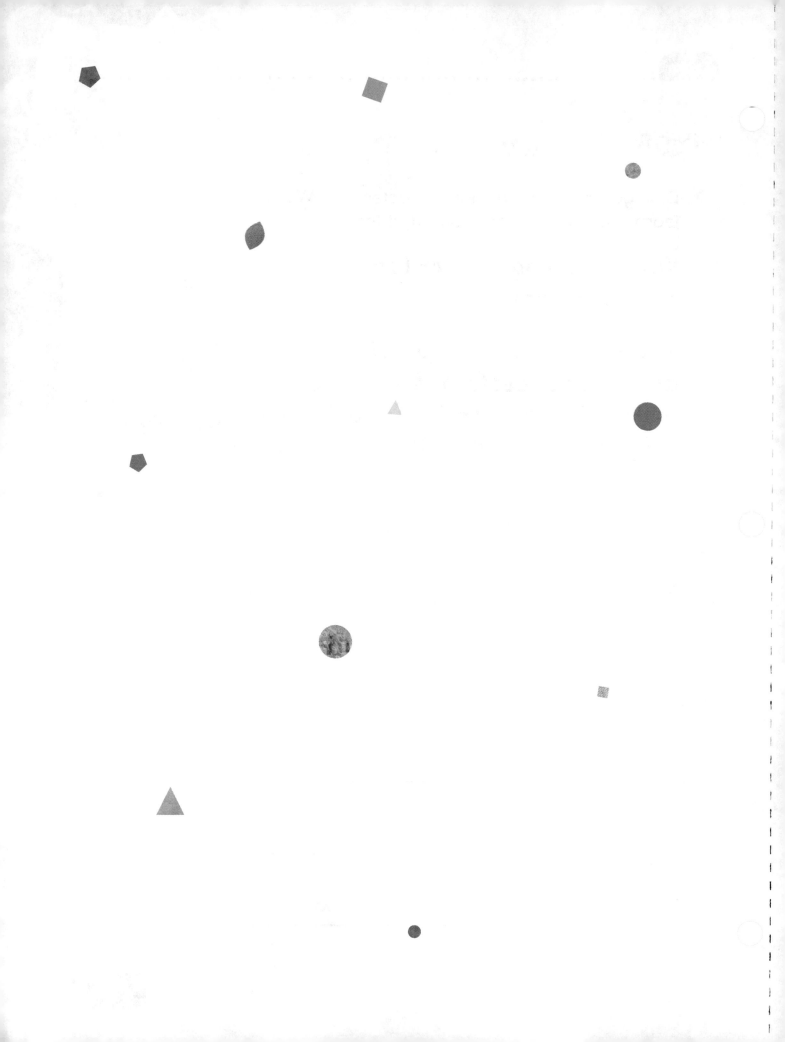

Draft a Story
Write a Story

Write a story. Be sure to use connecting words and order words from the word bank in your story.

> ### Word Bank
> | also | because | finally | later | so |
> |------|---------|---------|-------|-----|
> | and | but | first | next | then |

_____

_____

_____

_____

_____

_____

_____

_____

_____

_____

_____

_____

_____

_____

_____

LANGUAGE ARTS GREEN

Keep Writing Your Story
Tell Me About My Story

Have another person read your story and answer these questions.

1. What is the setting of the story?

_____

_____

2. Who are the main characters?

_____

_____

3. What is the problem in the story?

_____

_____

WRITING SKILLS

4. What is the solution to the problem?

_____

_____

_____

_____

5. In this story, what do you want to know more about?

_____

_____

_____

_____

Illustrate and Publish a Story
Check Your Writing

Answer the questions about your story.

1. Does your story have a problem and a solution?

   A. Yes   **B.** No

2. Are all the ideas in your story connected?

   A. Yes   **B.** No

3. Does your story have a title?

   A. Yes   **B.** No

4. Do you use order words such as *first, next, then,* and *finally?*

   A. Yes   **B.** No

5. Do you use connecting words such as *and, but, also, because,* and *so?*

   A. Yes   **B.** No

6. Do you begin each sentence with a capital letter and end with an end mark?

   A. Yes   **B.** No

Illustrate and Publish a Story
Publish Your Story

Publish the final version of your story and draw an illustration.

_____

_____

_____

_____

_____

_____

_____

LANGUAGE ARTS GREEN

_____

_____

_____

_____

_____